Cambridge Elements ≡

Elements in Publishing and Book Culture
edited by
Samantha Rayner
University College London
Leah Tether
University of Bristol

READING BESTSELLERS

Recommendation Culture and the Multimodal Reader

Danielle Fuller
University of Alberta
DeNel Rehberg Sedo
Mount Saint Vincent University

CAMBRIDGE
UNIVERSITY PRESS

CAMBRIDGE
UNIVERSITY PRESS

Shaftesbury Road, Cambridge CB2 8EA, United Kingdom

One Liberty Plaza, 20th Floor, New York, NY 10006, USA

477 Williamstown Road, Port Melbourne, VIC 3207, Australia

314–321, 3rd Floor, Plot 3, Splendor Forum, Jasola District Centre,
New Delhi – 110025, India

103 Penang Road, #05–06/07, Visioncrest Commercial, Singapore 238467

Cambridge University Press is part of Cambridge University Press & Assessment,
a department of the University of Cambridge.

We share the University's mission to contribute to society through the pursuit of
education, learning and research at the highest international levels of excellence.

www.cambridge.org
Information on this title: www.cambridge.org/9781108812931

DOI: 10.1017/9781108891042

First published 2023

A catalogue record for this publication is available from the British Library.

ISBN 978-1-108-81293-1 Paperback
ISSN 2514-8524 (online)
ISSN 2514-8516 (print)

Reading Bestsellers

Recommendation Culture and the Multimodal Reader

Elements in Publishing and Book Culture

DOI: 10.1017/9781108891042
First published online: April 2023

Danielle Fuller
University of Alberta

DeNel Rehberg Sedo
Mount Saint Vincent University

Author for correspondence: Danielle Fuller, dfuller@ualberta.ca

ABSTRACT: Readers are essential agents in the production of bestsellers but bestsellers are not essential to readers' leisure pursuits. The starting point in this Element is readers' opinions about and their uses of bestselling fiction in English. Readers' relationships with bestsellers bring into view their practices of book selection and their navigation of book recommendation culture. Based on three years of original research (2019–21), including a quantitative survey with readers, interviews with social media influencers, and qualitative work with international Gen Z readers in a private Instagram chat space, the authors highlight three core actions contemporary multimodal readers make – choosing, connecting, and responding – in a transmedia era when on- and offline media practices coexist. The contemporary multimodal reader, or the MMR[3], they argue, illustrates the pervasiveness of recommendation culture, reliance on trusted others, and an ethic of responsiveness.

KEYWORDS: readers, bestsellers, recommendation culture, influencers, multimodal reading

ISBNs: 9781108812931 (PB), 9781108891042 (OC)
ISSNs: 2514-8524 (online), 2514-8516 (print)

Contents

1 Introduction

Readers rarely identify bestsellers as their favourite type of book to read. Most readers, however, have an opinion about what a bestseller is, and, consciously or not, that opinion informs how they choose their next read. Consider the last time you saw, heard, or read the term *bestseller*. Maybe you were walking past tables piled with books in a bookstore and a cover sticker caught your eye. Perhaps you were waiting in line at the supermarket next to a rack of paperbacks with a bestsellers shelf label. You might have noticed the recurring image of a book cover while browsing your social media feeds. Possibly a friend passed along a recent read featured on several bestseller lists. Whatever the situation, your decision to ignore a bestseller or to take note, to click on a post or to swipe past it, suggests something about your reading habits, preferences, and selection practices. Adult readers' attitudes to the term *bestseller*, particularly bestselling fiction in English, and their relationships with anglophone reading recommendation cultures are the subject of this Element.

Our thesis is simple. Readers play a crucial role in maintaining the success and reputation of bestselling fiction. Without readers buying, borrowing, and recommending books, sales, library loans, and reader-generated reviews cannot exist in the quantities required to put a newly published book on a bestseller list or to bring an older, backlist title into the physical spaces and onto the virtual platforms where many readers go to discover books. What is more complex and interesting is how readers interact with the culture constructed around bestsellers by agents in the book industry and mass media, by social media influencers, and by other readers. In this short Element we present an analysis of original research that we pursued across three years (2019–21). While the commission to write about 'reading bestsellers' came with certain parameters – most significantly the focus on bestselling fiction in English – the focus on recommendation culture and the multimodal reader arose from our preliminary investigations into readers' understanding of bestsellers. In particular, readers' use of information about bestselling fiction foregrounded their position in post-digital book cultures, so that the question shaping our research became: what is it like to be a reader, not just in a transmedia age, but in an era when old and new media, on- and offline practices, coexist?

The main sections of *Reading Bestsellers* offer a snapshot in time of readers' opinions and actions that conveys some of the qualities of that experience.

We have also attempted to address some of the gaps in anglophone scholarship about contemporary readers and networked reading cultures. For example, rather than focussing on the material that Bookstagram and BookTube influencers publish, we asked them about their motivations, production processes, platform preferences, and sponsorship deals (see Section 3, 'Connecting'). In each phase of the research – quantitative questionnaire, semi-structured interviews with influencers, asynchronous Instagram group with sixteen young adult readers – we sought to elaborate how readers saw themselves as agents within the online and offline processes that generate bestsellers. We also wanted to understand how and why readers who were not influencers use different virtual and non-virtual sources for reading recommendations. We took an iterative approach to each of the phases, employing digital tools that enabled international participation. Of course, we could not address every aspect of contemporary reading cultures and there are skews and under-representation, not least because we conducted the research in English. Some who participated in our research thoughtfully identified its limits. As one reader succinctly wrote, 'The parameters that often make a "bestselling fiction" are not universal' (Momo, Instagram group member, 2021). Other readers in our study demonstrated through their reading practices, and also through their comments, how genre and generation, language and geography, gender, racialization, and class shape how and where readers recommend books. Participants also discussed privileges and structural inequalities operating at local, national, and transnational levels that shape access to books, other media, and the technologies that distribute and deliver them. In doing so, they pushed back against the categories of our research commission into reading bestselling fiction in anglophone markets.

Readers and Bestsellers

Everything is bestselling nowadays. A book is hardly going to be advertised as 'the latest underperforming novel from the author of some books that didn't do well and that you didn't read'. (Anonymous questionnaire respondent, Feb. 2020)

Most readers recognize 'bestseller' as a category created by book industry professionals to draw attention to particular books. The overt cynicism expressed by this anonymous respondent represents a view articulated by some of our readers. The category 'bestseller' reminds readers that books are commodities, notwithstanding their primary association with it: high-volume sales, or popular genre fiction authored by a highly successful writer (e.g., Lee Childs; Colleen Hoover), or a title that has received multiple literary prizes. As we examine in Section 2, 'Choosing', the tension between commerce and culture produces unease for some readers for a variety of reasons. At the very least, *bestseller* appears to be an unreliable signifier. A reader from the third phase of our research articulated this well: 'the title "bestseller" seems to ascribe some value to the book, so many people trust that if it's a bestseller, it must be a really good book (but maybe it is not?!)'. Uncertainty about what exactly is being signalled by the bestseller *badge* is the reason many of the participants in our research trust the assessments and reviews of other readers, especially if the recommendation is from a friend.

The *hype* about a work of bestselling fiction may begin with the *buzz* created by publishers milling about at the Frankfurt Book Fair, as vividly described and analysed by Driscoll and Squires (2020). Once the appellation of bestseller is made manifest in material form like a newspaper list, for example, it becomes a powerful paratext that can be used by authors, publishers, and booksellers in the marketing and selling of fiction. Sorenson (2017) conceptualizes this process in terms of 'positive-feedback market mechanisms ... which can cause a product's success (or lack thereof) to be self-reinforcing' (88). But where are readers in this model? Steiner's (2014) analysis of international megasellers, or 'titles that sell far more copies than most bestsellers', is useful in this regard (57). She argues that a bestseller must be 'understood as part of a complex system in which the particular work of fiction, serendipity, and clever marketing are equally important' (41). She defines serendipity in this context as readers' desire to share the experience of reading a text read by many, but calls for more scholarly attention to readers within that 'complex system'. As Steiner notes, readers' ideas about what constitutes bestselling fiction and how they use the marketing and other paratexts that surround bestsellers is largely missing from scholarship about bestsellers in English. Critical attention has been focussed on other issues like defining bestsellers (for a summary, see Wilkins & Bennett 2021, 5–7); deconstructing and critiquing the ways that influential bestseller lists are formulated (e.g., Childress 2011; Miller 2000); or predicting or identifying what factors will produce a bestseller (e.g., Archer & Jocker 2016). Surveys and histories of bestsellers in English tend to highlight books and/or authors rather than readers (e.g., Sutherland 2007). Meanwhile, several recent studies highlight the importance of digital formats, especially ebooks (e.g., McKinnon 2015), or the success of particular audiobooks (Weber 2019) to the creation of bestsellers. Some reception studies of individual bestselling books do analyze what attracts readers to them, helpfully demonstrating how, for example, particular themes and genres engage them (Driscoll & Rehberg Sedo 2018). Illouz's (2014) book about the megaseller *Fifty Shades of Grey* is notable for her consideration of the creative role played by readers in the production of the novel because of its genesis as fanfiction.

Illouz also highlights the important relationship between romance and bestsellers in the USA, where, at the time of her study, the genre accounted for nearly half of all mass-market paperback sales (13). Popular fiction genres like crime, romance, and fantasy dominate sales of bestselling fiction in English, regardless of format (Booknet Canada 2022, 18; see also 'Best Sellers – Books – The New York Times'). These genres are also read and enjoyed by many readers who participated in our research, often alongside literary fiction and non-fiction genres (see Section 2, 'Choosing', and Section 4, 'Responding'). Another marker of the success and visibility of popular genres is their remediation and adaptation. As Gelder (2019) points out in his Element, 'popular genres are more likely to be adapted more frequently and extensively because they already inhabit a heavily commercialized cultural field. A bestseller already implies a large readership and, especially these days, global circulation' (3). Gelder's attention to the production and popularity of three fantasy series that have been adapted for film and television not only excavates the political economy of transmedia bestsellers but it also underlines the attraction for some readers of an extended immersion in a fictional world. While avid readers may take the approach of 'first the book, then the film', as one of the Instagram group readers expressed it, all readers are consumers not only of books but also of other media products. In our efforts to examine readers' ideas about and uses of bestselling fiction we conceptualized these opinions and practices as part of engaging with the mediascapes and communication technologies that they were navigating (see Section 4, 'Responding').

The Multimodal Reader 'Cubed'

The reader participating in the reading recommendation culture of the third decade of the twenty-first century is a multimodal reader, or, as we have come to imagine them, multimodal readers 'cubed'. The MMR^3s read multimodally in three dimensions in an era when digital and print cultures coexist, when reading materials might be transmedia objects or codex books (but also exist in other formats), and various devices can be used to read them. The MMR^3s navigate post-digital culture or 'the messy and para-doxical condition of art and media after digital technology revolutions' (Andersen, Cox & Papadopolous 2014, 5). Rather than signalling the end of a digital era, the post-digital can be considered the 'second (or even third wave)' of digitization 'wherein digital and analogue book technologies exist with simultaneous relevance' (Dane & Weber 2021, 1). For readers with access to these technologies, post-digital book culture represents opportu-nities for choosing what to read, how or if they connect with other readers, and how they respond to books, other readers, authors, and publishers. The MMR^3s act and interact within a mobile, networked, multimedia environ-ment (Fuller 2019). Some of them may be prosumers (Bruns 2008) who create content regularly; others will skim that content, possibly leaving a small trace of their reading act in the form of a 'like' or an emoji depending on the platform and the affordances of the device they are using. Levels and intensities of engagement and participation with networked reading cultures vary according to the readers who were involved in the research for this Element, some of whom have access to online reading recommendation sites and apps but choose not to use them. Not all MMR^3s engage with post-digital book cultures in the same way.

As book historians remind us, multimodal reading as a communicative practice is nothing new (Ouvry-Vial 2019). Readers have long been multi-modal actors; they engage in modes of communication that are gestural, visual, audio, spatial, and linguistic (Serafini 2012). Not all modes are used by all readers in all situations. Some communication might be to share an experience of reading face to face (f2f) with a friend or book group, or online through the creation of an Instagram book review. Multimodal modes of communication are also discernible in historical examples of shared reading such as in the reading aloud practices of some nineteenth-century literary societies (McHenry 2002); in domestic settings where a print-literate reader reads aloud to a familial group who may not have the same level of literacy (Ghosh 2003) or, further back in time, during situations of public reading whether religious or secular, for example, in late antiquity (Moorhead 2010). How this multimodality is or was engaged by a reader varies depending on the material form of the reading matter, the reader's abilities, the reader's literacy competencies, and on the absence or presence of an addressee or audience. As this explanation implies, we conceive of both an act of reading and the 'event of reading' (Radway 1991[1984]) as a social process that 'is always a practice embodied in gestures, spaces, and habits' (Chartier 1992, 51). As we have argued else-where (Fuller & Rehberg Sedo 2013, 27–43), these social practices are shaped by what Long (2003) called 'the social infrastructure of reading' (8), which includes the institutions and industries that produce not only reading materi-als, but also social scripts about the value and purpose of reading.

Echoing Chartier's theorization of reading as a social process, Thomas (2021) describes the digital environment as one where 'reading is increas-ingly conceived as active and creative, and where embodiment and situat-edness are constantly being reconceptualised and redefined' (2). The MMR[3] is still a socially situated reader involved in reading as a social practice, but their habits of reading are shaped by a post-digital reality where analogue and digital technologies are often entangled rather than binary opposites. An illustration might be the ways that some readers use their smartphone to read a bestseller list in the digital version of a newspaper like *The NYT* then reserve a print copy of a bestselling novel at their local library, later posting their review on Goodreads using their tablet. Another aspect of the entan-glement is the prominence of reader-created visual images of codex books in piles or on shelves in posts on platforms like Instagram, and readers' bodies (sometimes signified by only a hand flipping pages of a book) appearing in their YouTube videos or TikToks in front of book displays in bookshops. The MMR[3] is not necessarily always a content creator in this latter sense, but these practices, the still and moving images, and the bodily gestures of readers form repertoires of multimodal communication that are legible to them.

The Reading Industry and Recommendation Culture

We have conceptualized the agents, institutions, and organizations producing and consuming events, cultural artifacts, and media as part of early twenty-first-century book leisure reading culture as "the reading industry" (Fuller & Rehberg Sedo 2013, 15–27). Some of the factors that characterized the reading industry of the early 2000s were media convergence, intersecting fields of production, and collaborations between managers working in commercial and not-for-profit agencies. We have also examined how the reading industry was shaped by late capitalism and the neoliberal cultural policies in the USA, Canada, and the United Kingdom that promoted 'the creative economy' (129–35), consequently putting discursive and political pressure on the cultural industries to undertake the labour of social and community support in the wake of funding cuts to social services (135–8). The 'business' of the reading industry as we then defined it was 'to make leisure reading entertaining' (18). Mass reading events or broadcast book clubs were among the reading industry's products. The reader was an active agent within the reading industry in that they were selective about how they participated in events, expressive of various kinds of pleasure (and disappointment), and often had different ideas about the kinds of community that form around a shared experience of book reading (214–42). Today, many of the agents and features of the reading industry are still recognizable from the noughties, but the ubiquity of recommendation culture (Van Dijck 2013, 40), smartphone ownership, and the proliferation of social media platforms where readers might find 'affinity spaces' (Gee 2004) or 'affiliative' connections (Zappavigna 2011, cited in Thomas 2020, 84–5) are three of the biggest changes to how the reading industry operates.

Not only can publishers connect with readers directly and immediately, in ways they were still struggling to identify during the early 2000s

(Fuller, Rehberg Sedo & Squires 2011), but the more economically powerful houses use complex algorithms to capture data about readers' book choices and reading habits and direct content to them. As Kirchenbaum and Werner (2014) note, 'even a mainstream piece of literary fiction . . . is released into the kind of networked media environment that characterizes our most mundane daily interactions' (425). In the contemporary iteration of the reading industry 'books have become transmedia properties, franchises spanning multiple formats, media channels, and distribution networks' (452). Meanwhile, readers have become more important agents within the reading industry because they consume across various channels, and many also circulate their reviews and opinions within networked communities that are entangled within the structures and technologies of a wider online recommendation culture (Fan et al. 2018; Goodrich & de Mooij 2014). These digital practices are of relevance to any examination of bestsellers, because, as Parnell and Driscoll (2021) observe: 'Bestselling books are entwined with a range of digital practices, users and algorithms, including those on Twitter, Facebook and Instagram; reviews and interviews on blogs, BookTuber channels and below-the-line comments on digital newspaper features. Each of these digital nodes is an internally rich and complex site of reception' (4). When we foreground readers and their actions rather than bestselling books and their reception, as we do in our analysis, we must query how offline recommendation practices relate to digital ones, and we need to problematize the agency readers have within reading recommendation culture.

Readers have more ways of sharing their reading than ever before, and they can create content that influences other readers around the globe, but they must also contend with direct and indirect forms of marketing online, with data harvesting, aggressive algorithms, and data surveillance. This tension between readers' agency as commentators on what they consume, and how those commentaries can be influenced and easily co-opted by for-profit organizations that produce and distribute media, is a recurring concern underpinning our analyses in *Reading Bestsellers*. Readers often perform unpaid and underpaid labour for the publishing industry. For instance, many readers contribute through review posts and through the sharing of content by reblogging and retweeting to the very hype and buzz that some of them also criticize.

Readers also frequently engage in online recommendation culture by employing fan-like practices. These include the use of emotive language and the expression of their passion for particular books, and also the use of hashtags such as #amreading and #bookstagram. The behaviour that the media industries require of audiences is underlined by Scott (2019), who writes, 'media industries operating within a convergence context need audiences to be active, to behave like "fans", but they would prefer prescribed modes of activity that are promotionally beneficial and not ideologically challenging' (11). It is not only the publishing industry that requires readers to contribute to the reading industry in this way, but also the owners and managers of the social media platforms where readers connect with each other. We might understand the creation of the BookTok Book Club in July 2022 as an example of how the managers of a platform made explicit the already existing (and highly profitable) relationships among BookTokers with millions of followers, the publishing industry, and the networked recommendation culture supported by the features and affordances of TikTok (TikTok 2022).

The cross-media and cross-platform aspects of reading recommendation culture and its role within the contemporary reading industry become more explicit through collaborations between successful influencers and streaming companies. For example, in May 2021, three English-language BookTubers, each of whom had more than 250,000 subscribers, were employed by Netflix to review the television adaptation of the bestselling fantasy series Shadow and Bone by Leigh Bardugo before its launch (Still Watching Netflix 2021). We can understand this event in terms of Murray's (2011) conceptualization of the 'adaptation industry', wherein an existing audience for a book is the target of promotion for a film or television series. We should, however, also consider the practices of each influencer's followers, the rhetorical and material efforts of the influencers to maintain connection with their communities, and the friendship among influencers that is explicitly referenced by all three participants in the video. Some of these matters are taken up in Section 3, 'Connecting'. Meanwhile, what about the readers who comment on this video because they trust these influencers? The intricacies of parasocial relationships online, the types of intimacy that social media affords, and the way that readers pursue their interest in specific writers and genres all demand further critical attention. To do this work, reading studies scholars need to make a turn from the study of reading communities meeting in physical spaces to, in Burek Pierce's (2020) words, 'fans, media, and online communities', in a move that should include a critical consideration of the 'infinite diffusion' of 'social [media] space' (8). In *Reading Bestsellers* we begin to attend to the former within the context of the latter.

While for-profit and for-promotion relationships between the reading industry and recommendation culture may appear to be structured through practices of co-option and commercialization and the avoidance of content and creators who are 'ideologically challenging', fan studies scholars would be the first to remind us to pay attention to the variety of behaviours that occur within fandoms and online reading communities (Busse 2017; Jenkins 1992). For instance, influencers and their followers on BookTube, Bookstagram, and BookTok do not only express their passion for reading and their excitement about specific genres and individual books; many also critique the over-representation of white, middle-class personnel in the English-language publishing industry, and the under-representation of minoritized communities and perspectives in the contemporary fiction that those same companies produce. Two campaigns that began on Twitter, #ownvoices (2015) and #weneeddiversebooks (2014), continue to highlight these issues and have been taken up by influencers and users across platforms. Moreover, some Bookstagrammers, BookTokers, and BookTubers, especially (but not only) those who identify as Black, Indigenous or as a Person of Colour, queer and/or disabled, create content that highlights books by writers from minoritized communities, critique cultural appropriation, and actively discourage their followers from reading the books of writers whose work reproduces racist or ableist and/or heteronormative stereotypes, tropes, and narratives. Since elite white agents have the most power within the reading industry in terms of both economic and cultural capital (So 2021), bestselling fiction in English often reproduces and exhibits the racism, classism, and heteronormativity that pervade many public institutions and commercial organizations as well as online spaces.

Two respondents to our online questionnaire who effectively flagged this formation commented, '[Bestsellers are] books that white people read'; they are 'Books about boring, straight white people who create their own problems'. In Section 4, 'Responding', we discuss in more depth how and why a group of young adult readers troubled the category and the contents of bestselling fiction on these terms.

Before you read on . . .

. . . we have a few points to make about the contexts within which we undertook our primary research and about the structure and style of *Reading Bestsellers*.

Most of the original research we undertook for this Element was conducted during the global Covid-19 pandemic. However, we have not written an Element about pandemic reading (Norrick-Rühl and Towheed 2022) or about the specific cultural practices associated with 'bookishness' (Pressman 2021) that the situation of lockdown prompted. We always planned to conduct our research with and about readers and their relationships with bestsellers online. In fact, the questionnaire was circulated and promoted for six weeks during February and early March 2020. Subsequently, a decision that we had made back in 2018 to conduct interviews with influencers remotely, and to experiment with conducting research with a group of readers on a social media platform where they also engaged with recommendation culture, proved fortunate. Nevertheless, Covid-19 did have its impact on the pace of our work, as well as on the cultures of reading and the creation of bestsellers that were the central topics of our inquiry. The experience of lockdowns and ill health, economic hardships, loss, grief, and social and physical isolation beset many populations, affecting the readers as well who subsequently participated in the second and third phases of our investigation between April and June 2021.

Of course, book buying and borrowing practices were materially impacted by the closure of public library buildings and bookshops. Online sales, doorstep delivery, curbside pickup, and sales and loans of audiobooks and ebooks were among the ways that readers obtained their reading matter (Knibbs 2020; Squires 2020). BookTok surged in popularity especially among younger readers who could use their smartphones to create content and to connect with other readers through short, often emotive recommendation videos (Armitstead 2022). BookTokers demonstrably pushed specific books like the young adult (YA) queer dystopia *They All Die at the End* by Adam Silvera and Madeline Miller's novel *The Song of Achilles* onto bestseller lists. But many readers found that they could not read books during periods of lockdown, and, even for those who continued their regular book-reading habits, television offered another way of consuming storytelling. The readers in our international Instagram group expressed reliance on streaming services as an important source of entertainment between March 2020 and May 2021, for example.

Another significant context for our *Reading Bestsellers* research was the increased activity and public awareness of the anti-racist and decentralized Black Lives Matter movement (founded in 2013) after the murder of George Floyd in the USA on 25 May 2020. Many Bookstagrammers responded to the protests and activism that occurred across the months of May, June, and July that year by producing reading lists of fiction and non-fiction by Black writers. Libraries, bookstores, and newspapers in various nation states also produced lists and displays that sought to highlight writing about racism, Black history, and Black cultures. These activities all drew readers' attention to specific titles, some of which had long been in print, while others were newly published in direct response to the wave of protests following Floyd's murder. As Dane (2023) demonstrates, however, *The NYT* bestseller lists from 2020 to 2021 show that the rise in sale of work by Black authors was not sustained (49–67).

While Black Lives Matter became a transnational movement, the uncovering of Indigenous children's graves in June 2021 at the sites of what had been residential schools sparked a campaign, Every Child Matters, that was more local to the lands on which the authors currently live and work. Once again, Instagram and TikTok were platforms where both Indigenous and non-Indigenous readers recommended books that critiqued the history of colonial violence, as well as novels, poetry, and short fiction by Indigenous writers that articulated stories of survival, resilience, and cultural resurgence. Some of these titles became Canadian bestsellers for a short time.

These two events foreground the appearance of transnational online reading recommendation cultures reflecting politics and social conditions in specific nation states or global regions. In this Element, there are moments when it becomes evident through readers' experiences and commentaries that some aspects of online reading recommendation culture alternatively obscure or foreground these specificities of location and situation.

In what follows, you will find an analysis of adult readers' attitudes to the term *bestseller*, more particularly to bestselling fiction in English, and their relationships with anglophone reading recommendation cultures. We have divided our discussion into three sections that highlight three sets of practices that readers in our study undertook or identified as part of their engagement with bestselling fiction in English and recommendation culture. As we hinted, these sections also take up different phases of our research investigation. Section 2, 'Choosing', focusses on the results of our internationally circulated questionnaire; Section 3, 'Connecting', on the motivations, labour, and recommendation practices of three influencers we interviewed; and Section 4, 'Responding', on the inter- and extra-group reading and media habits of the Gen Z Instagram group that we formed for the project. A discussion of the conceptual rationale for these section titles is included in the introductions to each. Finally, please also prepare to meet three readers: Sara, Priya, and Jana. They emerged from our data and sprang to life in our imaginations. They represent aspects of our analysis and animate specific ways MMR[3]s participate in contemporary reading cultures. Inspired by a mash-up of the case profile method (Yin 2017) with a television production process known as the Baltimore Method (Fuller 2019), these three readers and their everyday lives may also kindle ideas about MMR[3]s, recommendation culture, and reading bestsellers not fully articulated in this short Element.

2 Choosing

Sara locks the door to the archives and checks in her handbag for her phone, house keys, N95 mask, and paperback novel. All there. She glances at her FitBit, then takes the stairs up to the main foyer of the legal firm's glass-clad building. It feels good to stretch her legs after a day tethered to her desk, eyes glued to the computer screen. She blinks rapidly and reaches for her sunglasses as she hits the sun-drenched foyer. She must bring her eye drops tomorrow if she is going to continue working with that new cataloguing system! A quick wave to Frederika the receptionist and Edvin the janitor who are chatting at the front desk, and then Sara is propelled by the revolving doors out onto the streets of Stockholm. She veers away from her usual tram stop and walks rapidly towards Djurgården where she is meeting her book group at a café-bar. Her phone buzzes with a text from her friend Ann: 'Have secured table on terrace! Txt me ur drink order?' Sara smiles at her phone, fondly recalling the last book launch party she attended, courtesy of Ann's job as a publicity director at Norstedts Förlag. What was the name of the signature cocktail they had created to pair with the novel's plot about a murder at a bookfair? Ah yes, The Summer Colophon. Sara chuckles to herself recalling how excited Ann and her colleagues were to be promoting a book set in their own working world. She had fun that night hearing all the in-jokes the marketing team had used in the social media and poster campaigns. Those guys certainly put their literary studies degrees to good use with their clever taglines and appreciation for metafiction! Their quick wit seems to have translated into commercial success since the book was reviewed in Dagens Nyheter *and listed on the Svensk Bokhandel bestseller list for several weeks. Sara has also seen it prominently displayed in the city's bookshops. Although she knows from her student days working in Akademibokhandeln that publishers pay for endcaps and in-store promotions, she is, nevertheless, impressed at the media coverage Ann was able to secure for the novel and its debut author, a woman, like Sara, in her late forties. After meeting the author at the launch, and finding her friendly and intelligent but a little overwhelmed by the support given to her first book, Sara had made a point of listening to a couple of the radio interviews and she paid more attention to Instagram than she usually does. Even though murder mysteries are not a genre she especially enjoys, she had read her signed copy and posted an upbeat review on Goodreads. She is always ready to play her part in supporting Swedish writers!*

Sara stops walking for a couple of minutes as she texts back 'Tak. Aperol Spritz!' and then she quickens her pace, eager to sit down in the sunshine with her book group friends. They have been meeting every month for nearly ten years, but this is only their third time in person after two years of using Zoom, and it's the first month that it has been warm enough to sit outside and enjoy the long daylight hours that late June affords them at this northern latitude. In fact, they were lucky to squeeze this evening into everyone's schedules given how close it is to Midsommer. Sara knows the group will be in good spirits, anticipating upcoming trips to the countryside and the coast. She hopes everyone has read the book, a work of contemporary literary fiction about friendships translated from English, even if they have already streamed the television adaptation, something that she herself has resisted doing while her own ideas about the characters and setting are still fresh in her mind. She read the novel in three evenings and the copy in her handbag is bristling with sticky notes, a habit she has continued from her graduate studies when she spent hours developing complicated systems to record her reading and ideas – appropriate for her library science training, perhaps, but, on reflection, a little 'extra' as her teen-aged niece Wilma would say. She pictures the collection of hardback notebooks still sitting on her bookshelf with no trace of the now defunct database software programmes she tried out then. Sara doesn't really feel sad about that. According to Wilma, she could represent Sweden in advocating for open-access cloud computing. Actually, Wilma might enjoy this book if she could tear herself away from reading Young Royals *fanfiction on her phone. Sara must remember to pass this copy on to her at the weekend.*

Rounding the street corner, Sara is happy to see her drink lined up near the one available chair – the table is somewhat crowded with paperbacks, ereaders, and smartphones. They always have things to Google during their book discussions but otherwise adhere to a pledge to ignore their phones so busy family lives and demanding jobs do not intrude on their time together. Sara picks up her cocktail and gestures around the table: 'skål för vänskap!'

———

Sara stepped out of our quantitative data and into our conversations to become a reader we could vividly imagine. For us, she embodies key characteristics and habits of the MMR[3] as they appeared in our February 2020 survey. Sara reads on multiple devices, she employs a variety of methods for discovering and choosing books, and she shares her reading experiences with other readers both on- and offline. Like many of the readers in our study, she has a strong genre preference when it comes to choosing books to read for pleasure. Sara has some knowledge of how publishing works and is not easily influenced by the promotional hype around the next work of bestselling fiction; rather, she is inclined to be slightly suspicious of it. As someone living in the Global North whose first language is Swedish, she is keenly aware of the English language as a dominant factor in relation to which books become transnational bestsellers either in the original language or in translation.

In this section, we situate some of Sara's book choices and shared reading practices within the wider context of those adopted by readers around the world who responded to our Reading Bestsellers survey. We share our analysis of our survey results, reflecting on some of the differences and continuities with our earlier reader survey conducted in 2004–7. We focus on what and on how our respondents choose their books. We attend to whether bestselling fiction in English appears as part of those practices and habits of choosing. We contend that social practices of reading are not markedly different from the readers we surveyed in the early 2000s as part of our examination of mass reading events (Fuller & Rehberg 2013). Imagining Sara as a reader representing some of the key themes in our 2020 data thus combines with a comparison of some of the results from the two surveys conducted thirteen years apart. Doing so in the first part of this section helps to foreground both continuities and changes in the habits and practices of adult leisure readers between the first and third decades of the twenty-first century.

Overview of Survey Participants

Sara walked out of our survey data set of 3,027 readers and onto the streets of Stockholm for several reasons.[1] As a cisgendered white woman in her late

---

[1] We recruited through a convenience sampling method via our professional and personal social media networks and email. The compensation was a draw for 3 $100 (CDN) bookseller gift certificates. Questions were a mix of closed- and open-ended.

forties with a university education and a white-collar job, Sara represents one of the largest groups of respondents. Like Sara, 2,388 (79 per cent) of respondents identify as woman or girl; 521 (17 per cent) as man or boy. Less than 1 per cent identify as transgender, nonbinary, genderfluid, or gender-queer. Sara represents the largest age category of our readers: forty to forty-nine (659; 622 per cent). Indeed, 861 (37 per cent) of the 2,297 readers who answered the age question are between the ages of thirty and fifty-nine. Most of our survey respondents (1,391; 67 per cent) have professional or tech roles in their jobs, like Sara. Education accounted for 941 (31 per cent) of the readers' area of work, and like Sara, 1,790 (60 per cent) have a graduate degree. English is the top language to read in for our readers (2,881; 95 per cent), but they read in many languages. Nearly a quarter of them (669; 22 per cent) reported that they read in at least two languages. Like Sara, 259 respondents read in Swedish, but Afrikaans, Hebrew, and Croatian were also listed. Sara is inspired by one of the subsets of data that resulted from our convenience sample: Swedish is one of the official languages. Sara, like many readers in our data set, is a privileged reader who benefits not only from the 'social infrastructure of reading' in terms of her advanced tertiary education (Long 2003, 8) and ready access to physical libraries and bookshops in part because of her urban location, but also in terms of her access to the virtual world (Morley 2021, 33). Sara also has the time, money, and literacy competencies to engage with reading and book recommendation culture on various platforms. She is an avid reader in common with most of our survey respondents. Of the 2020 survey respondents, 1,320 (44 per cent) read for leisure between two and five hours per week, 913 (30 per cent) read between six and ten hours per week, and 486 (16 per cent) read for more than ten hours per week.

In common with many respondents to our 2020 survey, and echoing the results from our earlier study, Sara has 'trusted others' whose taste in books she has learned to rely upon. In contrast to our findings in the noughties, however, Sara's resources for discovering and selecting which book to read next have expanded exponentially thanks to Web 2.0 and the rise of 'socially networked reading communities' (Thomas 2020). Sara can use her smart-phone to check her Goodreads account, reserve a title at the public library, buy a book online or from her local bookshop, and message her book group. While some of these actions were possible in 2007, mobile devices were not common. The combination of portable minicomputers, the increased availability of Wi-Fi, streaming technologies, and social media platforms has resulted in an online book recommendation culture that is mobile, fast, interconnected, and international. Such qualities can produce feelings of 'ambient intimacy' among readers living at opposite ends of the globe (Reichelt 2007). However, alongside the opportunities afforded to readers to share information about and opinions of books on platforms such as Instagram, Facebook, and YouTube, are several barriers. The digital world replicates many of the cultural and economic inequalities of the offline world with regards to access to both hardware and broadband. As a middle-class woman with a professional income living in Sweden, Sara has reliable connectivity to the Internet and can afford up-to-the-minute mobile devices.

Sara's social practices of reading are inflected by her age and her lived experience of rapidly changing technologies from analogue to digital platforms, and by major shifts in delivery systems for entertainment whether the media object is a book, a film, or a TV show. As a Gen Xer, Sara is more likely to use Facebook than TikTok (Auxier & Anderson 2021), for example, and while she probably follows a few Bookstagrammers, some of whom are Swedish bloggers, she rarely writes in their comments. As a long-term member of a face-to-face (f2f) book group, Sara is also well versed in the interpretive practices of group-based booktalk (Allington & Benwell 2012). In fact, Sara's book club selects genres to read much like the individual readers in our data set. The top five genres selected by 2020 survey respondents were: contemporary fiction (2,167; 72 per cent), classical literature (1,321; 44 per cent), history (1,195; 39 per cent), mystery (1,188; 39 per cent), and autobiography/memoir (1,154; 38 per cent). Other genres of fiction accounted for what 455 (15 per cent) readers read most often, but it is notable that non-fiction genres – that is, those aside from autobiography, memoir, and history – were more popular still with 803 readers (27 per cent). The popularity of non-fiction genres within our own data set is reflected in the 'megaseller' success of celebrity memoirs (Steiner 2014) such as Michelle Obama's *Becoming* (2018) and Tara Westover's *Educated* (2018). Readers in our 2020 survey prompt us to remember that, although this current study has bestselling *fiction* books as one of its commissioned parameters, some readers might prefer reading non-fiction, while others read both. Moreover, just as readers help to maintain the reputation of fiction bestsellers, they also play a role in creating long-tail sales and library loans for non-fiction bestsellers by participating in book recommendation cultures.

How Readers Choose Books (Then and Now)

Regardless of readers' genre preferences, the top ways that readers choose a book to read are nearly the same in the 2020 data set as in our original study, as illustrated in Table 1.

The readers in our surveys are loyal to authors, and friend recommendations remain important.[2] Of course, in 2020 our respondents were more likely to follow an author online. Table 1 does not illustrate how a reader elicits or receives a recommendation from a friend, or whether 'friends' are known to the reader offline, online, or a mixture of both. Because both work colleagues and family members appear high on readers' lists we suggest that, in at least some cases, these sources of recommendation are f2f, especially given that our 2020 survey was conducted right before many people were subject to pandemic lockdowns. Intriguingly, there is a small decrease between 2007 and 2020 when it comes to bestseller lists as the most used means of selecting a book to read next. In 2007, 1,214 (35 per cent) of our readers noted that they turned to bestseller lists, whereas 890 (29 per cent) of the 2020 group used bestseller lists. The most obvious explanation is the proliferation and diversification of online 'list culture' since 2007 (Young 2017). Readers now have many more ways to navigate and identify information about books including actual lists produced by online influencers as well as the 'lists' suggested through influencer practices.

---

[2] We duplicated this question about choosing. There was an 'other' option. When the 'other' option was a platform mention, we adjusted the data set. Social media platforms were not part of the top five ways of choosing. In 2020, we added a specific social media platform question to the survey.

Table 1 Choosing what to read

	2020 N = 3,520	Frequency	Percent	2020 N = 3,027	Frequency	Percent
1	Favourite author	2,819	80%	Favourite author	2,224	73%
2	Friend's recommendations	2,775	78%	Friend's recommendations	2,165	72%
3	Family member's recommendations	1,782	51%	Prize winners	1,201	40%
4	Work colleague's recommendations	1,458	41%	Family member's recommendations	1,200	40%
5	Cover or jacket copy	1,457	41%	Work colleague's recommendations	1,070	35%

Other points of comparison between the two surveys highlight the influence of the reading industry that produces contemporary cultures of reading. For example, 2020 readers ranked prize winners as the third most frequently used method of selecting a book to read (Table 1). In 2007 it was also a highly employed method with 1,281 (38 per cent) of readers selecting this option. Prize culture, as many scholars have noted, is a means of legitimizing specific genres as literary (English 2002; Marsden 2020; Squires 2004). Book and author prizes are important to the reading industry to confer cultural capital on titles and individual writers, capital that is readily converted into its economic form thanks to mass media-generated publicity around long- and short-lists for prizes and award ceremonies, all of which is intensified by the circulation of lists and winners on social media platforms. Contemporary book publishers still pay for badged copies of the printed books and for special displays in bookstores as tangible signs of value. Not only are there even more book prizes now, but prize culture is used by agents in the reading industry, including publishers, cultural managers of arts organizations, and booksellers, for overtly political reasons to highlight previously under-represented writers from marginalized communities (e.g., The Writer's Trust McClelland & Stuart Journey Prize).

While prize culture has intensified with the changes in media technologies, other ways of navigating book culture have altered because distribution and delivery systems for entertainment content such as subscription services and streaming for television and film have changed readers' relationships with those mass media. In 2007 celebrity readers, dubbed 'national librarians' by Collins (2010) because of their role as cultural curators, were most likely to be personalities whose fame and audience had been built through television talk shows. Only Oprah Winfrey was identified by our readers in our 2007 survey with 848 (24 per cent) readers looking to the media mogul to assist with book choices, many of which, of course, became bestsellers in North America (Butler, Cowan & Nilsson 2005; Konchar Farr 2005). In 2020 the former titan of book selection had all but disappeared from our survey, replaced by Reese Witherspoon, Emma Watson, and Jenna Bush.

Traditional mass media associated with print retained its importance, however, as a source for book recommendations. Reviews by professional reader-critics in magazines and newspapers remained a significant way of choosing what to read next, although both were slightly less popular than in the 2007 survey. While 1,166 (33 per cent) readers used newspaper sections or reviews in the first survey, in 2020, 778 (26 per cent) readers chose that option; the results for magazine reviews were 902 (26 per cent) in 2007, but 489 (16 per cent) in 2020. These figures do not reveal *how* the 2020 respondents accessed their newspaper and magazine reviews. We suspect that many people use the online apps and websites produced by national and local newspapers and magazines around the world, rather than the print versions that would have been evident for the 2007 respondents.

Unsurprisingly, a greater proportion of readers in 2020 used 'websites, blogs and online reviews' (668; 22 per cent) than they did in 2007 (566; 16 per cent), although the less than 10 per cent increase seems low until we contextualize those responses with readers' other online practices. In 2007, for example, no readers chose 'search/browse the Internet' as a way of finding ideas about their next book choice, while in 2020, 1,681 (56 per cent) readers reported that they used 'social media' as at least one method of selecting books to read. The major change in readers' choosing practices between our 2007 and 2020 surveys is the overall increase in using online resources amongst which blogs, websites, and online reviews are now part of selection processes that are more embedded in networked reading cultures and thus less visible to most readers as individuated resources for information about books. Bearing these interconnected, recycled, and repeated aspects of reading recommendation culture in mind, let us turn to which social media the readers in our 2020 survey use for choosing (or rather as part of their mix of resources for choosing) their next book.

In Figure 1 we see how Facebook (35 per cent), Goodreads (30 per cent), Instagram (21 per cent), and Twitter (18 per cent) were the top four platforms. Recall here that Sara, who characterizes the biggest age group of respondents (forty to forty-nine) (22 per cent), also engages with reading cultures on Facebook, Goodreads, and Twitter. There are a few other ways that the age distribution in our survey data maps onto social media use. The next biggest age group is fifty to fifty-nine (20 per cent), who tend to use Facebook (Auxier & Anderson 2021). Reddit was only selected by 3 per cent of our readers, but given that we only surveyed adults from the

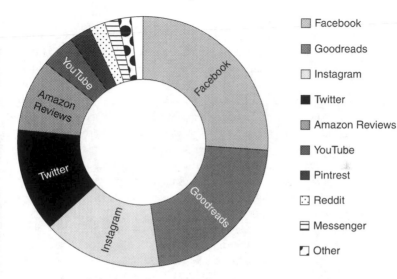

Figure 1 Social platforms for reading choices

age of nineteen upwards and the nineteen to twenty-nine age group represents 13.6 per cent of our data set, we should treat this result with caution because the largest percentage of users of Reddit are eighteen to twenty-nine (Auxier & Anderson 2021). Similarly, TikTok, another platform popular with youth, does not appear at all in Figure 1. BookTok, the TikTok subcommunity where readers share their ideas about books, rose rapidly in popularity during 2020 partly because of pandemic lockdowns and homeschooling that restricted the activities of many school-aged people. Wilma, Sara's niece, most likely scans BookToks to find reading recommendations, and Sara herself may encounter BookToks crossposted on Instagram.

We depicted Sara as a reader who would use her smartphone to check social media apps, search for information, and text with her friends. As a Scandinavian, Sara is almost always able to connect to wireless technology regardless of whether she is at home, at work, or in a public space (see 'Nordic Embassy – International Business Development Consultancy' n.d.). She has access to digital connectivity rivaled only by South Koreans. But does this encourage Sara to read digital rather than printed text or to use her smartphone rather than a codex format? Not necessarily. Most readers in our 2020 survey who were Sara's age preferred printed books for their leisure reading, but a significant number of them opted for ebooks on ereaders. Notably, in the youngest age group (nineteen to twenty-nine; n = 412), most respondents also chose paperback and hardbound books (261; 63 per cent and 146; 35 per cent) as their preferred devices with 82 selecting audiobooks. Interestingly, in our data set using ebooks was an especially popular way of book reading among those aged between sixty and sixty-nine (n = 434; 217; 50 per cent) with hardback books the next most popular choice (173; 40 per cent).

What are the implications of these results for considering how readers participate in contemporary reading recommendation culture? More specifically, what role do readers play in sustaining the shelf life and long tail sales of bestselling fiction in English? Contemporary readers have many more opportunities than they did before to share their ideas about books with others. To discover more about what these readers chose to share, and their attitudes towards bestselling fiction, we turn to the responses to our cluster of questions aimed at readers who at least occasionally read bestsellers.

Reading Bestselling Fiction

More than two-thirds of our respondents (2,068; 69 per cent) note they read bestselling fiction, at least occasionally. Of these readers, a staggering 80 per cent share information about it, indicating how readily 'the contagious talk' about a book that may begin as a conversation among publishers at an international book fair (Driscoll & Squires 2020, 17) operates on a much bigger scale once regular readers engage with it. The most frequently mentioned ways to share are with friends (1,489; 49 per cent), family (1,129; 37 per cent), and work colleagues (844; 30 per cent). As with the results for choosing the next book to read, we do not know whether this sharing happens f2f or online. However, given how we have characterized reading recommendation culture as involving both online and offline practices of choosing and sharing information, this distinction is not especially significant. Their 'networked reading' practices are not only employed and realized online using social media platforms designed to enable rapid and ephemeral forms of connection. They also practice 'networked reading' within their physically realized communities. Our readers confirm that f2f and virtual practices of social reading are both in play when it comes to communicating their ideas about bestselling fiction. Sharing their reading with their f2f book club is common (403; 19 per cent), while Facebook and Goodreads are the most mentioned platforms (403; 13 per cent and 419; 14 per cent, respectively). Given that most readers are especially likely to value a book recommendation from a trusted other, we can begin to comprehend how important the reader-to-reader commentary about a potential or actual work of bestselling fiction is to the amplification of 'buzz' about it. We can also grasp the importance of the contemporary reader as the MMR[3] who can share their choices across platforms through communicative acts that variously involve images, text, sound, and touch using a variety of communication devices and apps. The MMR[3] suggested by our data also, like Sara, communicates in f2f networks through direct conversation and, perhaps, through group booktalk.

What bestselling fiction were the readers in our 2020 survey choosing? The top five most-mentioned titles are listed in Table 2. There are several striking aspects. First, not all the books are fiction: three titles are contemporary literary fiction and two are memoirs, which suggests that not all readers were paying attention to the word 'fiction' and/or that some readers do not recognize the genre of memoir as non-fiction. Second, the books were written by cisgendered women, two of whom were already well-established as celebrities with significant amounts of social and cultural capital because of their political activities (Obama) and literary success (Atwood). Both women also have a substantial number of followers on at least one social media platform. The authors were already well-known personalities with an audience, important elements for making a book into a bestseller. Third, all the books were written in English and had publishers with a headquarters in an anglophone territory. All were also translated into multiple languages, making them available to readers in

Table 2 Readers' last read of bestselling fiction, 2020 survey

Where the Crawdads Sing (101 mentions)	Delia Owens	G. P. Putnam's Sons (USA) 14 August 2018
The Testaments (70)	Margaret Atwood	McClelland & Stewart (Canada); Nan A. Talese (US); Chatto & Windus (UK) 10 September 2019
Educated (37)	Tara Westover	Random House (USA) 18 February 2018
Becoming (30)	Michelle Obama	Crown (USA); Viking Press (Commonwealth) 13 November 2018
Normal People (26)	Sally Rooney	Faber & Faber (UK) 28 August 2018

multiple regions of the world; these books were able to move transnation-ally not only through online recommendation culture but also in a more material sense as physical objects (printed books) and digital formats in accordance with licenses and rights granted because of publishers' socio-legal negotiations. Fourth, all but one of the five books – *The Testaments* – were published at least eighteen months before we ran our reader survey, indicating that the list serves as a snapshot of a milestone in the shelf life of these titles. Readers may have known these books were bestsellers when they chose them and, by buying or borrowing them, they contributed to sales and library loan statistics even if they did not go on to recommend the book to others. Given that the top three ways for readers in our 2020 survey to obtain a work of bestselling fiction were the library (33 per cent), online bookseller (21 per cent), and chain bookseller (16.9 per cent), we note that, from the perspective of readers, 'bestseller' may connote a popular book borrowed and/or read by others as much as it might signal a high volume of sales.

Readers' perceptions about and attitudes towards bestselling fiction generate another set of issues that are worth some critical reflection. We asked respondents: when you hear, see or read the words 'bestselling fiction', which of the following ideas comes into your mind? (choose as many as apply). The options were an idiosyncratic blend of book genres, industry practices, and readers' responses, and they were randomized to counter any hierarchy that might be inferred from a list presented in an order decided by us.

Not surprisingly, many readers identified sales and lists based on sales among their associations. We have referred to these definitions as 'industry categories': the way that cultural managers in the book industry regard sales volume as a signal of success. Readers understand these ways of measuring 'bestsellers' even if, like 993 (33 per cent) of our respondents, they might also query the source, as indicated in the option 'Bestselling according to whom?' Similarly, the high position of 'Display in a Book Store' (1,214; 40 per cent) and 'Marketing' (1,189; 39 per cent) suggests that these industry practices are recognized by readers whether or not they prompt them to buy or borrow the titles. Notably, 1,979 (42 per cent) of our readers chose 'Famous Author' from the list as something that they associate with 'bestselling fiction', a result that coincides with one of the top ways that respondents choose their next book to read, and with the appearance of Margaret Atwood (and likely also Michelle Obama) on our top-five list of the last bestseller our respondents had read. While this indicates that publishers and booksellers are right to engage with author branding as a promotional practice, from a reader perspective it reminds us that books by 'favourite' and 'famous' authors pique their interest. In each case, the author's name connotes a degree of cultural legitimacy and offers the reader a level of reliability. Other popular associations were 'Books That Have Won Prizes' (1,066; 35 per cent) and 'Books You Can Buy from Pharmacy, Grocery Store etc.' (757; 25 per cent). While prizes usually connote quality because a book has been accorded critical acclaim by a jury, the second option is more readily associated with convenience of availability. Supermarkets and pharmacies that sell books usually reserve their shelf space for genre fiction by well-known writers produced in a mass market pocketbook format (see Figure 2).

From our own, unscientific observations during the three years of this study, we observed that a reader is more likely to encounter a 'Bestsellers' shelf label in a store that doesn't specialize in books than in a bookstore. Exceptions include airport bookstores (Figure 3). In both supermarkets and airports, readers may be in a hurry to make a choice, and in both locations, the primary reason for being there is not book-buying. For readers in these book selection situations, 'Bestsellers' operates as a literal label and book displays organized around high-volume sellers, famous authors, and prize winners help readers to efficiently navigate the selection of books presented to them.

Classification: 'Bestseller'

The quantitative data from the survey provide a bird's-eye view of respondents' perceptions of the term 'bestselling fiction', but it is the qualitative responses to the 'Other (please specify)' option of this question that provides nuanced evidence of how readers use the term to make choices. Among the readers who responded to this question, there was also a notable lack of ease with the classification 'bestseller'. Eleven hundred and seventy-six (39 per cent) respondents took the opportunity to write a comment. The following responses represent the most repeated descriptors and attitudes in our data set:

Figure 2 An Edmonton shoppers Drug Mart, November 2019 (authors' photo)

Something I might be interested in looking through
Marketing puff
Might be a nice distraction for the beach but it is often
   disappointing so not worth trying
Popular, good quality
Overhyped
I assume it will be good or easy

As this short list suggests, quality was a polarizing issue. For every 'good quality' remark, there is another reader for whom 'bestselling fiction' connotes 'not necessarily well written'. For every respondent who associates the term with mass appeal using a neutral or positive tone, for example, writing something like, 'Books that are read by a large public', there is

Figure 3 San Francisco International Airport May 2022 (authors' photo)

a respondent who understands that popularity as signaling a lack of sophistication in the reading public. A typical example is: 'pop fiction; lowest common denominator fiction'.

Within our collection of responses, there are many mentions of 'genre fiction'. Specific genres from 'sci-fi' to 'action' to 'thriller' are foremost in readers' minds when they consider their associations with the term 'bestselling fiction'. Since many of the comments about associations with the term were evaluative in tone, we organized them into three simple categories. The results were that 789 people (26 per cent) expressed a negative reaction to the phrase 'bestselling fiction', 689 (23 per cent) remarks were neutral, and only 364 (12 per cent) comments were considered positive reactions.

Negative responses to marketing practices around bestsellers that some readers consider suspect or 'overhyped' can actually add to the 'buzz' about a book when readers participate in online reading recommendation culture. When we tracked readers' talk about *Where the Crawdads Sing* across Instagram in October 2019, we found that resisting the marketing and media 'buzz' about *Crawdads*, or loving or hating Owens' novel, frequently signalled their reading tastes and also fuelled readers' curiosity so that millions of readers became sufficiently aware of the novel to consider buying or borrowing it. For some of our readers, any sign that a book is a 'bestseller' is a helpful navigational tool that can be used for pathfinding within recommendation culture. Uses of this tool vary: identifying 'light' reads or books to research more before possibly borrowing or buying; as an indicator of what other readers are reading because it is 'trendy', or as evidence that a volume of other readers purchased it.

Conclusions

As we have discussed, twenty-first-century readers from the noughties up to the early part of the pandemic continued to reference trusted others such as friends, family, and work colleagues as part of their practices of choosing what to read next. We conclude that social bonds that are shaped at least in part by shared taste play a significant role in building and maintaining the reputation of bestselling fiction. A significant difference in contemporary reading cultures between the 2007 and 2020 surveys is the direct involvement of the book publishing industry within reading recommendation culture, both in terms of the sponsorship of influencers and sophisticated computational systems that inform data-driven decision-making at the 'big four' English-language publishing companies. As Murray (2018, 2019) and others (Rowberry 2019; Smith & Telang 2016) have noted, data about readers are an asset. To underline this point, we note that book industry professionals from the major English-language publishers we interviewed in the noughties were struggling to find ways to engage with and influence readers who were meeting and exchanging information about books online, but, in the 2020s, that is no longer the case. Economic transactions between sponsors and influencers are openly acknowledged in posts and videos so that readers are aware when a free book, gift bag, outfit, or lifestyle product has been provided. Explicit recognition of paid for or partially paid for content may account in part for the high level of awareness among our 2020 survey respondents about the marketing practices of book publishers. That consumer savvy, combined with readers' varied and variegated strategies for choosing books, inflects their perceptions of and attitudes towards bestselling fiction. The unease that readers registered about bestsellers through their contradictory comments about quality remind us that the tension between commerce and culture – a tension evident in Leavis' (1977, 1932) early twentieth-century observations about readers and in our own analysis of readers' 'dance of distinction' (Fuller & Rehberg Sedo 2013, 76–90) – continues into contemporary book and reading cultures. The skew of our 2020 data set towards readers of Sara's age may partly be responsible for this, since the Gen Z readers we worked with in the third phase of research tended to concern themselves more with the politics of representation than with issues of cultural commodification or with cultural hierarchies of taste.

3 Connecting

If there is one type of reader who can create a bestseller, it is a social media influencer who recommends books. Often acting as a trusted other for avid readers who go online to seek out their next book choice, influencers have a significant role to play in reading recommendation culture by lending both legitimacy and visibility to the books that they review, discuss, and display across social media platforms. Making connections is central to the practices of reading influencers. Their work involves connecting with readers, with other influencers, and with professionals from the publishing industry. Connecting can be understood at once as a form of labour involving both paid and unpaid work, as a performance as an MMR[3] online, and as an affective and relational practice of 'loving a book in public' (Fuller & Rehberg Sedo 2013, 199–201). Influencers themselves may understand what they do in different terms and, of course, how they connect with other readers is also inflected by the affordances, features, and algorithms of the platforms they use (MacTavish 2021, 81). Nevertheless, reading influencers have created repertoires of practice and vernaculars of reading that have become normalized on platforms like YouTube since it was launched in June 2005, and on Instagram (launched in October 2010). BookTube and Bookstagram, the names given to the niches where reading cultures operate on those platforms, occupy us in this section because they are the primary platforms used by the influencers we interviewed. However, these are only two nodes in networked reading cultures that exist across the range of social media platforms from Reddit to Pinterest. As researchers of contemporary readers, we can safely say that if a platform can be used for booktalk, then readers will find it and figure out a way to share their reading experiences on it.

During the first stage of the global pandemic (2020–1), connecting with other readers and finding books to read as a form of escape, solace, and entertainment took on a new urgency for many readers (Anderson 2020; Boucher, Harrison & Giovanelli 2020; Dietz 2022; Squires 2021). In that context, the rise of BookTokers (Martens, Balling & Higgason 2022), who were most frequently teenaged and young adult readers making short videos on their smartphones, made headlines (Armitstead 2022; Beale 2022; Harris 2022; Wiederhold 2022). Publishers and booksellers were ecstatic because

BookTokers, who quickly garnered millions of views, sent readers into brick-and-mortar bookstores and drove traffic to online bookshops. Novels were propelled onto the bestseller lists, regardless of whether they were new publications or had been on shelves for years (BookNet Canada 2022; Flood 2022). For the reading industry, BookTokers have become, at least for now, the ultimate influencers whose social capital is highly valued. It remains to be seen how this commercial relationship will shape the genres of books that are published. What we will underscore here is that the connecting practices of BookTokers within reading recommendation culture online, are, in many regards, like those employed by BookTubers and Bookstagrammers. Aesthetics, formats, and vernacular practices differ across platforms, but the affective and relational aspects of communication are constant, albeit frequently intensified as the infamous BookTok tags 'books that made me cry', and 'books that Tiktok made me buy' vividly suggest (Harris 2021; C. Murray 2021).

In what follows we examine the experiences of three influencers who have become what used to be called 'microcelebrities' within online reading recommendation culture, but whom digital media studies scholar Abidin (2015) notes should simply be called influencers. These three influencers have gained credibility among readers because of their enthusiasm for and expertise about fiction. They have not garnered their cultural and social capital in another field of entertainment like the actor and film producer Reese Witherspoon, who hosts a book club across several social media platforms. Celebrity book club hosts can create bestsellers. Witherspoon's purchase of the film rights to *Where the Crawdads Sing* coincided with her selection of the title for her book club in September 2018, bringing it to the attention of many anglophone readers. Readers of this Element will recall that Owens' novel was the most mentioned work of bestselling fiction in our February 2020 survey. But what role do the avid readers-turned-influencers play in the creation or maintenance of bestselling fiction? How and why did they take their love of books online, and what do they understand about the community of content creators they encounter there? What changes have they experienced, and how have these altered their relationship with their followers, with sponsors and with books? This is a story told from their point of view and organized through the three themes that emerged from our interviews: serious conversations about books, authentic work, friendship, and community. Structuring our discussion of connecting in this way also foregrounds the norms, values, and practices of these influencers who participate in BookTube and Bookstagram.

Serious Conversations about Books: Influencers as MMR^3s

Ariel Bissett is a Canadian-based book influencer with a substantial following who was part of a group of readers in the earlier days of BookTube. She told us:

> I started making book review videos in 2011. At the time there were something like twenty channels that were dedicated solely to book content and they were all run by young women. I saw an opportunity to make friends and share thoughts about a hobby I loved and asked my dad (I was 16) to help me set up my YouTube channel and to borrow the family camera. In that early period the community didn't have a name ('Booktubia' floated around as a term, until the simplicity of 'BookTube' became solidified) and it copied a lot of the video trends happening in other communities. Unlike now, where YouTube is full of niche areas and communities (because so many users are on the platform so there is a big enough population for these niche genres to flourish), at the time it was a lot more independent-creator focused and decentralized. YouTube now officially recommends finding a niche community to flourish in when you're joining the platform. Interestingly, the book community found a lot of inspiration in the 'Beauty Guru' and fashion parts of YouTube. Videos like 'clothing hauls', 'product reviews', 'monthly favourites' and 'tag videos' were thriving there and similar content started happening for books. The simple foundational concept, reviewing books, remained the mainstay for a few years, but a lot of additional videos like book hauls, library hauls, monthly wrap ups and book tags also became popular.

Taking cues from Ariel's experience, one way of understanding the history of influencers within reading recommendation cultures online is to consider it as a story about avid readers who found a way of using platforms that, initially at least, did not necessarily lend themselves especially well to interactive booktalk. By experimenting with filming and editing, sharing tips with other readers on the same platform, and borrowing online practices from more popular communities of practice, readers who wanted to share their passion for books developed the competencies, skills, and content models required to attract and engage with other readers. Some of them, like Ariel, have accrued many followers and subscribers, at least in terms of the online communities around books where it is possible to become an influencer who attracts sponsorship deals with smaller-scale audiences than in other niches.[3] The three influencers we interviewed all make content for the English-language book community and were selected because they have three different levels of followers: 5,000–10,000 (@savannahbooks)[4], 20,000–50,000 (@jennareadsbooks), and more than 300,000 (@arielbissett). Each influencer has tried several platforms, sometimes diverting their time and energy to a different platform when new functions and features became available, at others, leaving a platform because of changes like a rise in the amount of advertising or algorithms that they experienced as disruptive to their ability to sustain a conversation about books.

At the time of the interviews (April to July 2021), all three influencers maintained active accounts on more than one platform, and each had a preference. In a networked online environment, the ability to connect and recirculate content across multiple platforms is important and is one way that influencers contribute to the creation of bestsellers, as we explore

---

[3] As way of illustration, consider that Cristina Riccio, aka Polandbananasbooks, has 428K subscribers on YouTube and 143K followers on Instagram (as xtinemay), and Jesse the Reader has 397K subscribers on YouTube and 151K followers on Instagram. Meanwhile, the top fashion influencer is Zoella Zeebo with 9.3 million followers on Instagram and 10.8 million on YouTube (influencemarketinghub.com).

[4] @savannahbooks is a pseudonym.

later in our discussion of authentic work. While we hesitate to over-generalize about the roles of influencers on the basis of three interviews, we believe that each interviewee offers significant insights into their own motivations and pleasures, production practices, and reading experiences. The perspective of the content creators themselves has frequently been absent from extant scholarship about Bookstagram and BookTube, where analyses of published content are usually critiqued in terms of aesthetics, rhetoric, and interpretive practices (Birke 2021; S. Murray 2018; Thomas 2020). Here, then, we begin to address that omission.

Influencers in the book community are often highly skilled MMR[3]'s who pursue multidimensional conversations about books. In common with many readers who become book group organizers or cultural managers of literature and reading programmes, however, they start making content because they love books and want to share their reading experiences with others. They practice 'loving a book in public', a description of a shared interpretive reading practice articulated to us by Jane Davis, the founder of The Reader organization in Liverpool, United Kingdom (Fuller & Rehberg Sedo 2013, 200). Davis was referring to a facilitated, group reading model that has been employed across a series of f2f settings, and a mode of social reading that has an explicitly healing purpose. While the modality of our interviewees' shared reading diverges from Davis' significantly, their motivation, and their belief that exchanging ideas and feelings about books connects people, is similar. Jenna described her work on Bookstagram thus: 'I don't think I'm a professional reviewer. I don't think of it as a job. I think of it more as, I want to share, I want to talk about these books with book friends and other book people who maybe have read this. Because the chances that somebody that I know in real life having read that book is low (laughter)'.

@jennareadsbooks is a North American Bookstagrammer in her early thirties who mostly reads and reviews 'straight up literary fiction'. When we interviewed her in April 2021, she had just finished Kazuo Ishiguro's novel *Klara in the Sun*. As the quotation indicates, her primary motivation for creating posts on Instagram is to exchange views about her reading with others who are similarly committed to books because she does not 'have reader friends' offline. Going online enables her to engage in booktalk, a practice that she pursues for pleasure. While she listens to many audio-books, she prefers to read paperbacks. Her preference for the codex is reflected in the many photographs of her bookshelves and bookstacks that appear on her Instagram grid. In common with many contemporary readers who alternate between formats, audiobooks enable her to walk the dog or cook dinner without interrupting her reading. But, unlike most MMR[3]s, Jenna is also directly connected to the production of audiobooks through her professional job as a software engineer for @librofm. Nevertheless, her salaried work does not put her under any obligation with regards to what or how she reviews books.

Jenna described how her vernacular practice aligns with her original pleasure-based motivations for starting her Bookstagram: 'I feel like I'm just word vomiting my feelings about the book and it's because I want to talk about it with people. But I want to have more of a conversation.' Although she started out posting once a day, @jennareadsbooks currently posts a couple of times a week and only about books that she is actually reading. With practice, her ability to create posts quickly ('10 to 15 minutes') has improved: 'It only takes me a couple of minutes to take a picture and then edit it,' she told us. The commentaries she writes typically run from 200 to 300 words, and, as she put it, 'I'm not a great detailed reviewer.' While the speed with which she creates posts and their length accord well with the original affordances of Instagram's image+text template, she has no desire to create Stories – a function that Instagram introduced in August 2016. Nor does she want to make Reels (on Instagram) or TikToks because she believes both formats require more set-up, filming, and editing time. For Jenna, then, discussing her opinions, feelings, and ideas about literary fiction with others is something both that she undertakes for fun and that she can do quickly. It is also a practice that she takes sufficiently seriously to post regularly. By September 2022 @jennareadsbooks had more than 47,000 followers, which in Bookstagram terms is in the middle-range size for an audience. At 40 K+, however, it is difficult to hold a serious conversation about books with so many people, the majority of whom are likely scrolling quickly through her posts. Typically, between ten and forty readers add a comment beneath Jenna's reviews indicating their intention to read the book, their disagreement or agreement with her assessment of it, or adding a recommendation for a similar title.

Like Jenna, Olivia-Savannah of @savannahbooks began sharing her love of reading publicly through a literary blog, a genre that predates social media and one that has been remarkably persistent in online reading and book cultures (Driscoll 2019; S. Murray 2018; Thomas 2020). Based in western Europe, Olivia-Savannah was in her early twenties when we interviewed her in May 2021, and she was completing an English literature degree at university. Although she 'doesn't really have a favourite genre', what she reads depends on her 'mood', for example, choosing a romance as 'a quick comfort pick me up', or alternating between YA novels and literary classics when studying for university is stressful. At the time of the interview, she was 'reading a lot of non-fiction' because she was 'enjoying learning'. She had recently read Tilda Shalof's *A Nurse's Story*, a book about the pandemic; *Dear Reader* by Cathy Rentzenbrink about 'how books have helped her through her life'; and *Brown Baby* by Nikesh Shukla, 'which is about growing up Indian British and trying to raise a Indian British child'. A keen reader from an early age, Olivia-Savannah was barely in her teens when she started to try out various online platforms where she could 'talk about books'. In her own words:

> It started with my blog. I was 12 or 13 and I just discovered book blogs and I was fascinated, I wanted to make my own talk about books online. And then I think after a few years somebody saw that I took photos of books and put them in my blog posts and they said, 'Have you heard of the Instagram book community?' and then I hopped over onto Bookstagram and I was there for a few years but kept my blog and at some point someone said YouTube was really taking off with books so I hopped over there and now I just do all three.

Maintaining a presence across three platforms is time-consuming, and over the years she has allowed the blog 'to become my smaller platform', hosting only occasional posts rather than the two blogs a week that she wrote as a high school student. Time is not the only factor shaping her platform preferences, however, since she derives different benefits and pleasures from creating content for each platform:

What I most enjoy about Instagram would have to be creating the pictures. I have a lot of fun making the photos and I find it very therapeutic and calming. And then having an online platform to put them on is kind of an excuse to be making these photos of books, which I'm not sure what I would do with them without it. And then for YouTube, I would definitely say it's the conversations, it's the comments, it's the interactions that I really value. And being able to discuss books in detail with other people or someone picks up a book and they get back to me and they said they really enjoyed it for whatever reason. I really like that about the YouTube platform.

In common with Jenna and Ariel, Olivia-Savannah values the opportunity to exchange ideas about books with others. Her YouTube videos generally include detailed evaluations of several books and involve her speaking directly to the camera with very few animations or fast edits. The slow-paced style and longer running times (many of her videos are at least thirty minutes long and occasionally run more than an hour) are reminiscent of earlier BookTube videos rather than the more slickly produced and edited short-form videos (ten minutes and under) that are more typical of BookTube in the 2020s. That said, Olivia-Savannah also engages with the now-established BookTube genres of book hauls (when a reader introduces a pile of recently acquired books), unhauls (getting rid of unwanted books), wrap ups (eg., all the books read in the last month), book challenges (eg., reading a book a day for a month), TBR (talking about a reader's To Be Read pile), best books of the year, focussing on a book genre (eg., gothic fiction), or promoting books by authors from marginalized communities or that represent or explore the experiences of people of colour (e.g., 'recommending books by Black authors with Black characters'). These videos, which are often shorter than 'review' videos, are clearly categorized and organized on her YouTube channel. With just over 6,800 subscribers, Olivia-Savannah has a small-scale following in BookTube terms. However, she has a faithful group of core followers who comment — often in detail with time stamps referencing specific ideas — on her videos, responding to her assessment of particular books, pledging to read a recommended book or sharing their own ideas about a book that they have also read. These are the 'conversations, comments and interactions' that she enjoys and finds motivational.

Ariel added another perspective when she explained why book content on YouTube can hold people's attention. Her commentary underlines some of the qualities that make a BookTube channel popular and hints at the dynamics of creator-audience relationships where the audience may be small, but the style of the video and the books featured have become familiar and 'make sense' to those watching:

> YouTube, and photo/video content in general, is highly curatable. The truth is that content creators on these platforms don't need to make sense to everyone, they only need to make sense to the people that watch them. While many might be surprised that hundreds of thousands of people (sometimes millions, in some exceptional cases) are willing to sit through a thirty-minute video about books, it happens! It's a testament to those creators. They are making entertaining, thoughtful, engaging videos that revolve around books, to whatever degree, and people are watching. Most of the videos that fit into this category are not droning discussions about the ins and outs of one book. They will have a fun hook, an interesting premise, maybe will be filmed in multiple locations or focus on multiple books, but the thread is simply that people enjoy watching.

Ariel's emphasis on fun and entertainment suggests why 'hundreds of thousands' of people might watch a video and choose to subscribe to a BookTuber's channel. Her own channel had more than 290,000 subscribers in August 2022 and a video that had been posted for a month had already received 65,000 views. Older videos from a year ago had higher statistics ranging from 72,000 to 121,000 views, indicating that some subscribers might not watch new content as soon as it is uploaded and, of course, it is possible that some viewers may be rewatching. It is common for

Ariel's book videos to attract more than 500 comments within a month of being posted. Followers interacting with the channel frequently praise Ariel's ability to hold the viewer's attention, her knowledge about a variety of genres of fiction, her 'love for books', and the ease with which she connects themes, critiques, and ideas across the featured books. Commentators interacting with Ariel in this way demonstrate their own passion for reading and knowledge of books through shared recommendations and literary quotations. Other viewers who write a comment use the affective language that is common online when users wish to show their appreciation, typically versions of 'Loved this!', while others address Ariel directly by name. She often replies to a few comments, thereby shifting what might be understood as readers' parasocial relation with her to one of interaction and direct connection. In this way, even a BookTuber with many followers can maintain at least a semblance of conversation with readers when a sustained, interactive, 'serious conversation about books' is no longer realizable at scale.

Olivia-Savannah's love of photography is evident and explicitly bookish themed on Bookstagram. As Thomas (2020) has demonstrated, 'the engage[ment] and play with books and book-related objects' (72) on Instagram illustrates 'social media's return to the "aesthetic of bookishness"'(Pressman 2014, cited in Thomas), and 'a response to the seeming dematerialisation of reading on digital devices'. The images in @savannahreadsbooks' posts exemplify these aesthetics with a mixture of bookstacks that are often balanced in her arms; flat lays of a book positioned among an assortment of other material items; a single book juxtaposed with a plant, flowers, or objects that share the colour palette of the book's cover; outdoor shots of a book held up against a complementary landscape; and upper-body shots of herself holding a book open as if she is reading it. As this brief list suggests, the photos are highly stylized and well designed, and they follow the visual genres that have become normalized on Bookstagram (Jaakkola 2019; Rodger 2019; Thomas 2021; Tselenti 2020). However, the appearance of the influencer's body and the photos which, although clearly posed display her as a reader, remind the viewer that there is indeed an actual, embodied, individuated reader making the photographs. Although these book-associated selfies are also part of an established repertoire of reader representation on Bookstagram, depicting the face or even parts of one's body in photographs or videos always involves a degree of risk, not least because it makes the content creator more easily identifiable offline. In such circumstances, the practice of 'loving a book in public' can place an influencer in a vulnerable position if followers – even the most well-intentioned book fans – misinterpret the 'perceived connectedness' (Abidin 2015) of online interaction as consent to approach and talk to a content creator in an offline space.

There are also risks of trolling and hate speech in online spaces. The risks are heightened for members of marginalized and/or racialized communities in online spaces that have been created and structured through technologies and regimes of power that have white masculinity encoded or 'baked in' (Chatelain 2019; Kim et al. 2018). However, influencers' actions, activism, and content challenges those dominant power structures and pushes back against the norms perpetuated by, but not always made explicit within, white, middle-class, feminized spaces of book groups (Ramdarshan Bold 2019). It is important to recognize the tenacity of whiteness in online spaces and the persistence of structural racism and the technologies that can, for example, make work by BIPOC writers and content creators less visible or searchable (see Parnell 2022). It is also important to consider the agency and actions of influencers in the 2020s who play a part in reconfiguring those spaces and norms.[5] Olivia-Savannah's self-presentation as a young Black woman reader circulates within an English-language book community where BIPOC influencers operate at all three levels of follower numbers that we outlined earlier, for example. Their content, their connections with each other, and their relationships with publishers and sponsors make a difference, not least in terms of encouraging BIPOC readers to participate in online reading communities. Moreover, as Jenna put it, 'hard conversations' about the politics of representation within books and the book industry can and do occur online. For the three influencers we interviewed, structural racism and diversity within the book industry, but also within

---

[5] See Boffone and Jerasa (2021) who write that the #DisruptTexts and #OwnVoices hashtags are part of a movement on Tiktok creating representation for those who may not see themselves in the books studied at school.

their own community of online creators, had become an especially important part of 'serious conversations about books' since the international Black Lives Matter protests during 2020.

Authentic Work: Managing Connection and Making Bestsellers

When we asked the influencers about whether they could create a bestseller, they each gave a similar response. They believed it was unlikely that an individual influencer could make a book into a high-volume seller, unless the influencer on those platforms led a celebrity book club. Nonetheless, all three influencers believed that, collectively, through many members of their creator community reviewing or featuring the same book, a bestseller could be made. Jenna reflected:

> I think Bookstagram as a collective could [create a bestseller]. If everyone was reading and posting about the book, I think that it definitely could ... it's hard to know what happened with *Where the Crawdads Sing* ... I will say it was all over Bookstagram. It's not my taste and I know I wouldn't like it if I read it, so I haven't. But it's one of those that I saw, I mean, it just dominated Bookstagram for a long time.

Jenna's commentary parallels our own observations about the recommendation culture around Delia Owen's bestselling novel, namely that it is difficult to establish who or which agent – for example, the publisher, Reese Witherspoon's book club, or an individual Bookstagrammer or BookTuber – began the chain of posts that led to the book's high-level profile on Instagram. What is identifiable, however, is that influencers on Instagram helped to maintain the visibility of the novel for a long time. As Jenna pointed out, 'if [a] book gets picked up by a lot of Bookstagrammers ... you're seeing it over and over and over and over and over, then somebody is more likely to buy that title'. The insights that influencers offer about their own work practices suggest how 'going viral' operates when it comes to making or maintaining a book's bestseller status.

If they are to buy, borrow, or reserve a book at a public library, readers who use social media may need to encounter content about a book multiple times, across different platforms, and on at least some accounts or channels curated by their preferred creators, or 'trusted others'. The visibility of a specific book can also be enhanced through the sub-network influencers like our interviewees have created across the platforms they use. Influencers deliberately establish a sub-network of reading communities by connecting their accounts on different platforms (Burek Pierce 2020, 74–8) through the functions that each platform offers, such as tagging, hashtags, and hyper-links, and also by recirculating, reblogging, or promoting content from one platform to another. These time-efficient practices of connection increase the likelihood of a reader seeing a review post or recommendation, which helps to create a bestselling book.

The effectiveness of influencers' connecting practices are not the only aspect of their work that contributes to the visibility of a potential bestseller or to the long-tail reputation of bestselling fiction. Their role within recommendation culture and the qualities of the labour that they undertake – work that has both paid and unpaid elements, and both commercial and affective effects – is crucial to the credibility of their reviews and recom-mendations. Influencers producing content for BookTube and Bookstagram are not only producers (Bruns 2008) but also 'cultural inter-mediaries' (Jaakkola 2022; Reddan 2022) connecting their followers to each other and to the reading industry. Book influencers punch above their weight relative to the numbers of followers required for social and com-mercial success in other online recommendation cultures, which is why an influencer with a small-scale following of 6,800 on YouTube like @savan-nahbooks is sent advance reader copies (ARCs) by publishers.

As MacTavish (2021) notes about Bookstagram, 'a small tier bookstagram account has the potential to emerge as a leading cultural mediator through niche content creation and a supportive community of supportive followers who engage frequently and in-depth' (85). Book influencers exercise author-ity as expert readers and trusted others within a recommendation culture where knowledge accrued through a combination of formal education and extensive and intensive reading practices is highly regarded. For the book influencer's work of evaluation and cultural mediation to remain appealing and authoritative, however, it must appear 'authentic' and 'genuine'. These terms were employed by the three interviewees themselves, but they are also part of an established discourse within communities of online content creators, especially on YouTube (Burgess & Green 2018, 95). When we asked our interviewees what makes a good post, Jenna responded, 'Well, it doesn't have to be anything special. I think for me, posts that I feel are good are more genuine, they're people actually talking about a book they read, versus just posting a pretty picture of book mail.'

As this statement indicates, not all posts or videos feature books that the content creator has actually read. Sometimes this is due to the pressures of making frequent content to retain the attention of followers and to 'feed the algorithm'. Influencers may use a genre like the book haul or TBR pile to indicate that these are books they are intrigued by but that they are not yet ready to evaluate. As Jenna pointed out, an influencer does not always explicitly say why they feature a book in a photo on Bookstagram, yet a reader-follower who is familiar with the influencer's reading tastes may notice a misalignment with their usual content. The practice can risk disrupting or breaking the influencer's role as a trusted other.

Of course, some forms of paid compensation are not as visible or as legible to readers who are followers. Similarly, book influencers with many followers are sometimes invited to be paid experts on panels at book industry conferences, at Videocons, or other types of fan or 'maker' conventions. These aspects of paid work are not a reliable form of income for producers, but they are opportunities that usually generate more interest in someone's channel or Bookstagram from readers looking for a trusted other; from journalists tracking trends in the book and media industries, and from industry professionals looking for influencers who can connect effectively with readers. Honesty about sponsorship through explicit statements and platform-featured labeling, and/or the use of a function that clearly generates income such as the paid-for content Ariel makes on Patreon, are ways influencers can balance the commercial aspects of their role with the work of cultural mediation. In this respect, an influencer can become explicitly involved in the promotion of a potential bestseller by framing their post or video as publicity for a book, and by acknowledging that it is an ARC from a named publisher. In common with all three of the influencers we interviewed, Jenna regularly receives ARCs from publishers who hope she will promote a forthcoming book. She pointed out that 'most review copies are sent no strings attached. You don't have to post on a certain day. There's no expectation that you'll post at all'. Both Jenna and Olivia-Savannah will ask for payment for a post or video if there are requirements about posting. In general, however, Bookstagrammers do not often receive monetary compensation from publishers. Olivia-Savannah remarked that payment from publishers depends on the platform and it is 'more so for YouTube, than Instagram. It's quite rare for Instagram'.

Notably, all three interviewees receive other free items as a form of sponsorship, including clothes, eyewear, bookshelves, and tea. Each influencer has explicit values around the type of sponsorship they will accept. For Olivia-Savannah, the ethics of a company's labour practices is a deciding factor. Meanwhile, Jenna honestly acknowledged that 'If I really want the product or want to try it, I probably won't ask for payment.' Neither influencer depends on their content work for their entire income, so they can pick and choose from the many requests they receive. Such non-book transactions are part of an economy in which expertise as a reader and acting as a trusted other has a commercial value that can be leveraged by publishers and also by marketing executives from companies producing other types of goods. As Burgess and Green (2018) note in their analysis of YouTube as 'a cultural space', 'the competing logics of expertise, authority, and value' place pressure on influencers who 'need to balance authenticity, intimacy and community' in their work as producers (22). Arguably, this is especially tricky on Instagram, a platform that has become highly commercialized through advertising and infamous algorithmic manipulations, 'making it into a marketplace for attention and commerce' (Leaver, Highfield & Abidin 2020, 4).

In Olivia-Savannah's description of a successful post on Bookstagram, she makes a clear distinction between two types of posts: sponsored and unsponsored. Some of her content is primarily for her followers, while some is publicity for a book and therefore part of a marketing campaign:

> I feel like a successful post for me has interaction, whether
> that be via comments or via somebody going through direct
> message saying that they are interested in a book. Or, if for
> example, it's a review copy and a publisher appreciates the
> post, they say they like it, or they say they want to reshare it,
> or the author themselves, I consider that a successful post.
> I think especially when the community interacts with the
> post but even more so when the publisher or author does
> because that's kind of who I'm doing it for and I know that
> it's reached them and it's been effective.

This commentary identifies a recursive element to the way communication
works within reading recommendation culture, marked by a successful
publicity post reaching the publisher or author of the book. Without further
investigation, it is difficult to assess how exactly an author or publisher
reacting to or recirculating influencers' sponsored posts and videos
increases the visibility and reach of a potential bestselling title. What we
can say with more certainty is that an author's involvement through a direct
comment or repost can reinforce the authority and credibility of the
influencer with their followers, and may, if the author is already well
known, bring the frisson of celebrity endorsement.

Ariel's reflection on changes in BookTube practices between 2011 and
2021 offers some insight into how a BookTuber might manage the 'competing logics of expertise, authority and value' (Burgess & Green 2018, 122),
while maintaining authenticity and engaging with the attention economy on
that platform:

> Perhaps the most surprising change has been that book
> review videos are very rarely made and always perform
> very badly in terms of views and engagement. While this
> was the mainstay for the early days of book videos, there are
> many factors that have changed their popularity. A creator
> must read a book in order to film a video for it, which is
> a time-consuming process, the book must be popular
> enough that many people will have already read it and are

therefore interested in hearing thoughts about it, or are very interested in eventually reading it, and it must be timed well and released during the popularity cycle of the book. These videos still happen but are packaged very differently. For example, videos with book lists like 'Reading X Celebrity's Favourite Books' doesn't sound like a book review but the video will still have the creator reading and reviewing books. The clever twist is that there is a bigger hook that appeals to a larger audience (everyone who likes or is interested in that celebrity), and the reviews can be snuck in, usually while you watch the creator doing other things too. This is not unique to the book community – especially as YouTube grows, it becomes more competitive, and creators must be creative in how they package and deliver their content to entertain their audiences.

Ariel's reference to the importance of timing and to the popularity cycle of the book suggests the significance of an influencer's knowledge of their role as an agent within the wider economies of book production and marketing to the success and impact of their evaluation of a book. Their ability to contribute to the creation of a bestseller is thus linked to their expertise and skills as a producer, to their relationships with publishers, and to their ability to navigate the competitive arena of their preferred platform.

Ariel is one of a small group of BookTubers working in English who earn most of their income from their online recommendation content. While these practitioners can leverage their cultural authority and social capital to help a book become a bestseller, they can also use their channel to spotlight books that may not receive much publicity. In doing so, a BookTuber reaffirms their knowledge and expertise as a reader and thus reinforces their role as a trusted other for their followers. For Ariel, such work involves the pleasures of browsing in bookstores, and the excitement of sharing a book with other readers, both aspects of book culture with which most avid readers can closely identify. She remarked:

I really enjoy recommending and reviewing lesser-known books on my channel because I know how difficult it is for books from unknown authors or authors from small publishers to get recognition. I don't aim to review a book *because* it's from any particular author or circumstance, but I enjoy finding diamonds in the rough when I'm in a bookstore and then that reflects in my videos and podcast. It's exciting to recommend people a truly great book that they may not have heard about before.

Conclusions: Navigating Connections

Considering the role of book influencers from their perspective foregrounds some of the materialities and technicalities of their labour and helps us to elucidate how they can play a significant part in the creation of a bestseller. Their commentaries also demonstrate that, despite the challenges involved, all three of our interviewees continue to enjoy their online work. Some of the pleasure they derive from it is via a sense of connecting with other readers through shared reading, but they also articulate a sense of belonging to a community that is constructed through different levels of connection and offers varying degrees of intimacy. There are the readers whose participation in reading recommendation culture involves 'liking' or 'commenting' on content, and perhaps some direct interaction with them as a creator, for example. But there are also friendships among influencers that exist publicly through tagging practices and direct interactions on each other's accounts, and that sometimes result in collaboratively made videos, podcasts, and posts.

All three interviewees referenced connecting with other influencers privately either individually or within online groups set up to share information about technical or commercial aspects of their work. But it is also evident that some friendships have extended into offline get-togethers, which are sometimes shared publicly through group photographs on their accounts, and, at other times, kept entirely private. The blurring of the boundaries between private and public, colleague and friend, fun and work, hobby and profession, appears to thread through the connecting practices of community for the influencers we interviewed. Their ability to navigate these relationships adds a further dimension to their work.

Connecting with a substantial audience of followers brings additional challenges and risks that can disrupt the intimacies of 'perceived connectedness' (Abidin 2015) that are possible at a smaller scale. Ariel offered these thoughtful reflections:

> At 20 k subscribers there was a sense that I had created a successful project. There were plenty of people watching my channel, I felt like I was part of the community, and I was able to work, in small but exciting ways, with publishers and authors. The realities of having a large audience are that people will begin to dehumanize you, criticize you, and feel distant from you. While nothing has functionally changed from how I created my videos when I had a smaller channel (I still film, edit, and upload everything on my own), the perception of me as a creator has changed. People will refer to me in the third person in my video comments, people will say rude things in my comments, both of which were things that didn't happen when I had a smaller channel. While I am very grateful for my channel growth I do have a lot of nostalgia for the days when the community and my channel were smaller.

The connecting work of book influencers must involve practices associated with book culture in both the online and offline worlds for them to appear authentic. Their content must demonstrate consistencies in terms of their reading tastes and/or interpretative practices, while also remaining entertaining and informative. Bookstagrammers and BookTubers can help to propel a book to bestselling status, but they also (crucially) make a notable contribution to the maintenance of a book's reputation across time and platforms. While influencers' promotion of specific books that they have received free from publishers is an integral part of the commercial economy of reading recommendation culture, influencers must balance it (and any paid-for content) with their own selections to maintain the trust of their followers.

Their passion for reading and excitement about books is required: they must remain authentic and genuine in their online work. Often highly skilled content creators as well as being widely read and educated, book influencers are avatars for their followers. They are a maxed-out version of the contemporary MMR[3]. With their ability to connect content and readers across platforms, and through their involvement in marketing books, they mediate between a community of reader-followers, the reading industry, and the economies of online platforms. It's not an easy gig.

———————

Priya checks her make-up in the mirror, then steps back into the apartment to see whether the outfit that a sponsor sent her to wear tonight needs an accessory. All good. It's something Priya genuinely likes, or she wouldn't wear it: the cut of the pants is flattering and the turquoise colour of the shirt looks amazing. She snaps a couple of mirror selfies just in case she needs them later for Instagram – not her favourite platform, but Cole might make a Story as part of their collaboration and a couple of behind-the-scenes shots could help drive some traffic towards it. Or she could edit them into her next video, perhaps. What else does she need to take to the pier gig? Phone, portable ring light, purse. Priya pauses outside the door to her bedroom and doubts start to creep into her mind: what if the music is too loud, the crowd too large, or she gets stuck on her own without Cole? Ugh. This is why she has a love/hate relationship with the media industry. In her day job, Priya can always hide behind her co-workers at events or give out the swag bags, but when she ventures outside of her bedroom and the safety of the tightly packed bookshelves to create content for her BookTube channel, she feels vulnerable. Ah yes, the book! It's a music gig primarily, but the soundtrack for the TV show wouldn't exist without the adaptation of the novel, so surely taking a hardcover book along won't look too out of place, will it? Too OG nerdy? Or is that some kind of oxymoron?! In any case, books and what they have to say about them are why they have both been invited, so the book must come to the party!

Priya grabs her signed copy of the novel and tosses it into the branded tote bag from the publisher, clutching the straps like they are a lifeline. She reread most of the novel last night, skimming through it to remember more detail: it's been more than a year since she read the ARC and reviewed it as part of a themed video on highly anticipated books with BIPOC representation, and she wanted to feel prepared. Even so, she would probably have refused the invitation if Cole hadn't suggested they go together. Cole loves meeting new people and is always the one in their friend group suggesting meetups and trips to bookstores. Before the pandemic he was even planning a tour of Europe so he could visit Bookstagrammers and BookTubers outside North America. Priya wishes she had half of Cole's social ease. He has that white cis-boy confidence going for him. (He would add 'exploded out the closet wearing glitter' confidence). He owns it, though, and he isn't a jerk. Priya's parents assumed he was her boyfriend because they appear together so often on Priya's social media feeds, until she explained that Cole is gay, which prompted another round of questions and explanations about queer identifications. Her parents are supportive of everything she does and wants to be, though, so Priya is grateful. They even helped financially when she moved to LA six years ago after completing her English studies degree.

Priya casts an eye around the shared apartment to see if she has left anything behind. Then she checks again: book, phone, ring light, purse. Okay: all there. It's doubtful that anyone will ask either Cole or Priya in-depth questions even though they are the two most-followed book influencers going to the gig, not least because their podcast really took off during the 2020 lockdowns. Priya's mind starts to go into overdrive: what if the author is there and they can film a quick Q&A for BookTok and maybe even set up a date to record a podcast episode? Priya rounded out her homework last night by jotting down a few pithy, well-informed questions just in case. Now she begins to hope that the author really is going to be there, although admittedly it's a long shot, given today's tweet about serving on that big prize jury with hundreds of books to read and a tight deadline. The price of bestselling success these days seems to be more work for the author; work that doesn't leave much time for writing another book. Especially if the author is Black, Indigenous or a person of colour. Or a woman. Or queer or disabled. And/or all and any of the above. Still, despite the demands and even given the racism online, Priya would gladly switch places with her favourite writers. Maybe if she can get some editorial help with her manuscript, that day is not so far off.

Priya gives herself a mental shake and takes a deep breath. She checks the time on her phone: better book an Uber now. She's allowed plenty of time to get from Inglewood to Santa Monica, but you never know with LA traffic. A quick DM to Cole and she's ready for whatever the evening brings.

4 Responding

Without readers there are no bestsellers. Or, more accurately, if readers do not buy and borrow books, there are no statistics to propel bestsellers onto lists. Without readers participating in online recommendation culture, whether by liking a post, writing a review or making a comment, or using a common hashtag like #currentlyreading, the buzz created around a book by publishers and influencers fizzles out. This much is evident to anyone who has been observing book and reading cultures on social media platforms over the past fifteen years. Meanwhile, signs and displays in physical bookstores highlighting 'BookTok selections' underline how significant the publicity and reader activity on that platform is to the selling of traditionally published books in the early 2020s. But how and why do readers navigate and negotiate with on- and offline recommendation practices, and with co-extensive print and digital media that provide potentially overwhelming information about books? More specifically, how does a generation of readers deemed *digital natives* respond to bestselling fiction in English, especially when English is not their first or only language? Indeed, how transnational is bestselling fiction in English from the point of view of readers in different regions around the world? Our curiosity about these questions, and our determination to work with a diverse group of readers aged nineteen to twenty-six years (Gen Z), living across five continents and in both the northern and southern hemispheres, inspired our creation of a private Instagram group. Through their discussions, posts, reactions, and reviews in the group chat, the multilingual, multiracial, all-gender group of sixteen readers demonstrated their familiarity with contemporary book cultures and with genres of reading practices on- and offline. Their actions and voices demonstrate and our analysis that follows underlines how central responding and being responsive are to their practices, ethics, and relationships with books and with other readers.

Within this group of avid readers, responding operates and can be conceptualized in several ways. They are highly responsive to the transmedia environment and media ecologies with which they engage; and they respond intellectually and emotionally to book recommendations, to the books that they read, and to each other. Their practices are, as the participle 'responding' implies, relational and dialogic: always involving a person, media object, or action. The group responds affectively, cognitively, and politically to bestsellers, to media, and to the world they live in. Enthusiasm for and pleasure in reading are shared values for these readers, but they do not especially care about bestsellers. Instead, they are exercised by issues of representation within books, motivated by global and local politics to find books that could deepen their understanding of various issues and systems, and they are fans of particular fiction and non-fiction genres. As we examine in this section, their responding practices are social because they are affective (passionate, eager), informed (by situated knowledge, geopolitics, and access to various media), and relational (interpersonal within and outside the group). Responding has both private and public virtual dimensions; the readers maintain accounts on multiple social media platforms. All group members had existing relationships with trusted other readers both on- and offline, demonstrating the post-digital nature of contemporary reading recommendation culture (Cramer 2014, 13; cited in Dane & Weber 2021, 1).

In this section we focus on the process of choosing a work of bestselling fiction to read and review for our Gen Z readers. We do this not to repeat our analysis of choosing practices derived from our quantitative survey, but rather because of what this aspect of the research foregrounded about MMR[3]s, recommendation culture, and bestsellers. The group was skilled at navigating online culture. The challenge of choosing a work of bestselling fiction in English revealed not only how they usually select books and use reading recommendation cultures, but also how and why they adopted additional, sometimes different practices to meet our request. The tensions in the commission for this Element you are reading emerged here, namely readers' fraught relationship with bestsellers as an industry category, their suspicion of the publicity around bestsellers, and the ubiquity of bestselling books for readers using both on- and offline tools for book discovery. Other tensions include the dominance of bestselling fiction in English over bestsellers in other languages, the structural constraints on how books do and do not move physically across political borders, and the extent to which bestselling fiction in English appeals to and represents readers across cultures and nation states. As Driscoll and Squires note: 'Bestsellers trave globally through rights deals across multiple territories and formats. Bestsellers also depend upon the generation of word-of-mouth marketing' (Driscoll & Squires 2020, 7). Readers are crucial to the latter process but may not always be able to participate because of legal, economic, and political impediments to media access and the flow of consumer goods. Working with these readers during the global pandemic (May–June 2021) made some of these constraints on their capacity to respond and be responsive even clearer.

———

Slightly out of breath after taking the stairs, Jana flops into the seat at their favourite desk in the library. With a view onto campus, the smattering of natural light available on this grey June day will at least help them to stay awake through their revision session. Jana takes a sip of their coffee and carefully sets down their reusable cup. They pull what they need out of their backpack: ring binder, notebook, textbook, highlighter pens, sticky notes, laptop, phone, and earbuds. They set up their study playlist on Spotify, then they arrange and rearrange all the other items on the desk until they achieve optimum work mode. All good. They power up the laptop, open the textbook, and find the relevant tab in the ring binder: 'Intersectional Feminism in a Global Context'. Jana begins to reflect on their different studying practices last semester when they felt like they were living permanently inside a Zoom room at home in Malaysia, literally and metaphorically removed from their fellow students in Melbourne. As their concentration deepens, a sense of relief washes over them: they have understood and remembered more than they imagined could be possible. Jana knows they have neglected their studying somewhat during the past eighteen months, escaping the pandemic and social isolation by reading audiobooks and borrowed paperbacks when they should have been focusing more on the course materials. Still, it seems that all that binge-reading of fantasy series recommended on Reddit, combined with con-siderable amounts of fanfic on AO3, and yes, watching a long lineup of Netflix series, several of which were adaptations of the books they had just finished (!), has not really impeded their university career. Too bad they aren't being examined on fantasy! Maybe they can find a course next semester about popular culture or genre fiction.

Jana pauses, picks up their phone and skims quickly through the university calendar. A sudden vibration alerts them to a notification from one of their group chats. Their friend Claire has sent a link and ☺. Claire is a student in the same programme as Jana and their go-to friend for recommendations about books, especially any kind of fiction, so if Claire thinks this panel discussion about inclusivity in publishing is interesting, they are going to seriously consider attending. The link leads to an ad for an event taking place on the campus and it's free, but it's the fact that their favourite indie bookshop is involved that catches Jana's attention. Even though they don't have much money to spare for book-buying, they really love browsing the shelves in the shop and noting down the staff recommendations. It's an amazing bookshop. There's always a prominent display of books by local writers and one of the biggest selections of LGBTQIA+ fiction and non-fiction that Jana has ever seen anywhere. Jana sends a thumbs-up and taps out 'studying rn', before putting down their phone and turning back to the laptop screen and binder notes. They can Google the panel participants later. One of them sounds familiar, though – maybe they have a YouTube channel or a TikTok. Or did they see their memoir in the bookshop? Whatever. They can go down that rabbit hole later. Jana picks up their phone to check the time: they can get in three solid hours of work before their shift at the cafe begins. Jana nudges up the volume on their music, picks up their pen and returns their attention to their lecture notes.

Introducing the Gen Z Reader Group: Responding to a Research Invitation

Like Jana, most of the young adults who joined the Instagram group had been studying online during the previous eighteen months.[6] Their experiences of remote learning, combined with their familiarity with Instagram and other communication apps, meant the idea of an asynchronous private chat group on

---

[6] We recruited through Instagram, Facebook, and Twitter. Our success, however, is due to our regional liaison colleagues in the Society for the History of Authorship, Reading and Publishing who invited their students to participate through email. We paid for the book that each participant chose to review and they were compensated with a book gift certificate.

Instagram was undaunting. When they responded to our recruitment ads, most of them expressed excitement about the international aspect of the group, their curiosity about our research, and their love of reading. Sixteen readers completed an online questionnaire as part of their participation in this piece of research, thirteen of whom were still active in the group at the end of the eight-week project. We asked them a range of questions in the survey about their reading preferences, media habits, and social media use, and we reprised the questions about bestsellers we had posed in our larger survey. In May 2021, the readers were living in Australia (three), Bangladesh (one), Canada (one), China (one), Germany (one), India (one), Indonesia (one), Jamaica (one), Mauritius (one), South Africa (two), United Kingdom (two), United States of America (one). Six of them were twenty-two years old; the others were nineteen to twenty-six. Eight read only in English and eight were multilingual. Most of the group identified as cisgendered men (three) or women (twelve) and one person identified as transgender. The participants used a mixture of forms of identification when asked about their ethnicity, some that were racialized, some nationalist, and one person combined nation state with a religious faith to which they are no longer affiliated.

In May 2021, twelve of the readers were full-time students and two were studying part-time. Four of the students had a part-time job, like Jana, but unlike them, several people were still studying remotely because of continuing entry restrictions as the result of Covid-19. We've imagined Jana to be studying and working on campus at the University of Melbourne in June 2022 after these restrictions were lifted in Australia. However, Jana's reading and study habits, their political interests, and their use of both digital and analogue devices and materials are inspired by our Gen Z readers. Most of our group of sixteen read across formats: e-book (ten; 62.5 per cent), paperback book (fifteen; 93.8 per cent), hardback book (eleven; 68.8 per cent), and audiobook (four; 25.0 per cent). In common with Jana, they read using a range of devices, depending in part on whether they are reading for pleasure or for educational purposes. These responses resonate with larger contemporaneous studies of readers undertaken in the USA (Noorda & Inman Berens 2021) and in the United Kingdom (Dietz 2022). Nationally focussed surveys by agencies such as BookNet Canada (2020) and The PEW Research Center (Faverio & Perrin 2022) also indicate that our Gen Z readers are typical of their age group in these habits and practices. They are the consummate MMR[3]s, using different devices, platforms, and formats according to their reading needs, but, given a choice, they will opt for a paperback or hardback book for pleasure reading.

Like Jana, most of the readers in this group use both offline and online recommendation strategies for finding their next book, but one reader had stopped using social media completely. As we discuss in what follows, a more nuanced picture of how they discover and obtain books emerged when we asked them to identify a bestselling fiction book (in English) that they would like to read and review.

Bonding: Responding to Each Other

All our participants had an Instagram account prior to our creation of the Reading Bestsellers private chat group, so they understood the functionality of the platform, its affordances, features, and genres of communication. Nevertheless, we were surprised at how they leapt into lively conversation about books immediately, in a way that indicated their knowledge of the language and style of reading recommendation cultures. Their excitement about meeting other young adults from around the world who shared their passion for reading shaped their ability to form interpersonal bonds quickly. They also understood the exigencies of a 'chat' group and combined short-form text with emojis to express emotions ranging from enthusiasm to self-deprecation of their own book nerdiness, often using the 'like' function to communicate support, interest and/or agreement (see Fuller & Rehberg Sedo 2023). This latter function was especially important in an asynchronous group chat whose members lived across many time zones. A typical session for most participants involved scrolling up to see what had happened while they had been sleeping or working before responding with 'likes' and emojis (especially smiling and laughing emojis) to various posts, and then maybe adding their own textual response to either a prompt question from us or a comment from one of their peers. The anonymized screenshot presented in Figure 4 depicts some of these practices as they appeared on the first two days. Bella, a twenty-year-old British woman in her final year of university, was exchanging recommendations based on recently read books with BeamingDays and @chooks. Their ability to summarize content or their affective reading

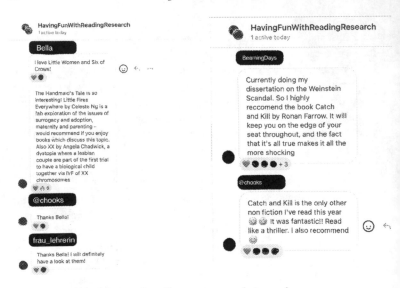

Figure 4 Early evidence of reading recommendation culture

experience or to use genre markers to convey briefly yet vividly how and why a book is worth reading suggests that these are styles of recommendation they are accustomed to sharing either privately with friends or, in the case of Bella, who runs a Bookstagram account, more publicly.

While eight group members participated in the chat more than the others – a common dynamic within any 'focus group' (Krueger & Casey 2009, 121) or informal book discussion (Peplow et al. 2015) – the asynchronous aspect removed some of the pressure to participate daily or to do more than 'like' a comment if they were pressured for time or had nothing to add to the conversation. Members were invited by us to answer questions and to undertake specific tasks. Nevertheless, as the screenshot demonstrates, the readers' interests in specific issues and genres and their willingness to share and recommend books that they were currently reading or had recently read, combined with their familiarity with the online chat format, resulted in exchanges that were ~ocial (affective and relational) and informal in style. They connected through ideas about books as well as the sharing of select information about themselves and their everyday lives. Bonding happened quickly, but it happened within the framework of a virtual private space created for research on Instagram, where offline identities were deliberately protected by pseudonyms. The participants' own awareness of how to present an online persona was employed within their responses to each other. Some of the readers chose to share one of their social media accounts that contained photographs of themselves, for instance, while others did not.

Navigating Book Choices: Responding to a Media Ecology

> I just finished reading a manga – 20th Century boys by Naoki Urasawa. It's about this group, who as kids during a summer vacation come up with scenarios where they save the world from evil, and as adults actually find their make believe stories coming true. And I have Six of Crows by Leigh Bardugo lined up. I got to know Netflix picked it up and a friend told me the books were good, so . . . 🐛 (Momo, 23 years old, India)

Befitting the generation that coined the euphemism 'Netflix and chill', the streaming service and other subscription delivery systems peppered nearly every phase of the group discussions. Like Momo, who lives in India, most of the participants had access to Netflix, excepting the reader in China, but the content that was available to each reader differed because of Netflix's licensing agreements. Momo's commentary highlights the various ways into book discovery that she commonly employs, indicating that a combination of news about a TV adaptation plus a recommendation from a friend informed her choice of Bardugo's novel, a bestseller especially popular with Gen Z readers and widely reviewed across social media platforms including TikTok (Armitstead 2022). This sense of books as media objects situated within a media ecology of platforms, products, and technologies and navigated according to tastes, economic resources, energy level, and mood, was common among group members.

Favourite fictional genres for TV and for books also emerged. Fantasy and dystopia are understood by these readers as cross-platform and cross-media entities, as well as books that may employ different forms, such as comics and prose fiction. These Gen Z readers are active participants in the genre worlds of crime, romance, and fantasy created by the 'social and industrial circulation of genres' (Wilkins, Driscoll & Fletcher 2022, 168). Their 'visible pleasure' in and enthusiasm for popular genres are not only produced from the 'textual conventions' of the media texts that they consume, as Wilkins and colleagues argue, but were also evident in and generated by the sharing of their experiences of media consumption. These sharing practices were recurrent in the group chat, often without any direct prompting from us. Pleasure emerged as an important value for the readers as a reason to recommend media texts to others, but the act of sharing itself also generated pleasure. This pleasure can be understood as belonging to the 'overall sociality of . . . genre worlds' (139), but, we contend, it is also a social pleasure derived from moments of interpersonal communication that were sometimes about identification and that, at other times, registered as curiosity and interest: a pleasure of responding in relation to others. Moreover, the Gen Z readers derived pleasure from recommending both popular and literary books, and, indeed, all kinds of media texts if the texts had created a sense of personal enjoyment. The pleasure might arise from being immersed in a fictional world, being informed about a real-world event or issue, or having an opportunity to engage with a text in its various multiple media formats. Notably, given our focus on bestselling fiction, books adapted for television shows that were available internationally via streaming services came to the attention of our readers. Some of these books were bestsellers prior to adaptation and saw increased sales afterwards; others became bestsellers because the adaptations were in circulation on a platform like Netflix. In Figure 5, for example, frau_lehrerin, a twenty-two-year-old living in Germany, is reading a bestseller with a widely watched television adaptation (*The Handmaid's Tale* 2017), and their TBR pile also includes a widely distributed production of a book adaptation on Netflix. She does not, however, specify whether she is reading these bestsellers in English or in German.

   Even though most of the group shared frau_lehrerin's preference for 'first the book, then the movie', they were curious about and likely to engage with adaptations and to seek out reviews of books, films, and television shows on social media. There is some resonance here with Hill's (2019) analysis of contemporary television audiences and their

HavingFunWithReadingResearch
1 active today

I'm currently reading The Handmaid's Tale by Margaret Atwood. I like dystopian novels very much and find it very interesting to "travel" to such imaginary worlds (especially as it is the only kind of traveling one can do right now...)
If I'd rather read something "lighter" and more relaxed, the first part of "Bridgerton" is also on my nightstand right now. My best friend loves the series, but I'm more of a "first the book, then the movie" type , so I haven't seen the series yet

❤●●●+ 4

Figure 5 First the book, then the movie

engagement with mediascapes. She writes, '[P]eople roam around story-telling within cross-media content. A key question to ask is what sort of movements become possible for roaming audiences in contemporary mediascapes?' (30). As committed book readers, our group appeared to roam across media using pathways and signposts that had already proven effective in leading to (book) content they enjoy. Their movements through mediascapes as book readers were guided by their genre preferences and especially influenced by friend recommendations and favourite authors, which were their top two ways of selecting their next book to read. Their methods of book discovery influenced how and where they roamed and, while they watched various types of shows on subscription services, from popular reality series like *RuPaul's Drag Race* to serial detective shows like *Lupin*, they generally chose these because they mirrored their favourite genres or they represented political and ethical issues that concerned them.

When they wrote these comments, Momo and frau_lehrerin were responding to our request for the group to share a typical post that represented their usual means of finding books. Some readers chose to write about their sources for book discovery, while others pasted or linked to a post from an influencer or a Goodreads review that typified their usual go-to sources. Most people in the group had one or two 'trusted others' on Bookstagram, BookTube, or podcasts, and would combine paying attention to their reviews with friend's recommendations. The group also considered school requirements, jacket copy, and covers. These features are a useful reminder of two aspects of the 'infrastructure of reading' (Long 2003, 8): education and the book industry. Proscribed reading often looms large in students' lives, taking up time and influencing their attitudes to reading, both positively and negatively, and, similarly, the material properties of a book can elicit a curious response or disinterest (Gilbert & Fister 2011). In terms of genres, history and contemporary fiction were the most popular in this group (nine readers chose one or both), with YA and classical literature almost as popular (chosen by eight readers). The latter two are key genres on Bookstagram (Thomas 2021), so these choices are not surprising given that the group consisted of readers familiar with Instagram. Our Gen Z readers, however, also enjoyed romance and poetry. As Burek Pierce (2020) comments in her examination of the fan readers who follow the Green brothers' multimedia content, 'for all the existence of bestsellers and broadly conceived market categories like fiction for young adults, readers, even those with an interest in popular materials, have varied rather than purely homogenous tastes' (100). The variety of genres the group enjoyed, combined with their roaming practices across the mediascape, suggests how differentiations between popular and high culture are not especially important to them. While these readers understood that prize culture, educational institutions, and traditional professional newspaper reviewing contribute to a cultural hierarchy of value among book genres and, indeed, among media practices, their own movements among media and genres disrupt those processes of evaluation and stratification.

Responding to Reading Recommendation Culture

Avid readers, the Gen Z group are not dismissive of traditional mass media when it comes to book reviews. Their usual practices of selecting a book are as heterogeneous as their taste in genres. Rather like a flat lay of objects in a Bookstagram post, these readers gather various types of information about books, from diverse media sources on- and offline, as if they were making collages of possible content choices. Their book selections are often made through lateral connections prompted by repetition across media, through friend recommendations, and because of algorithms that curate what they see on their social media feeds. As Jamaican reader @chooks wrote about her choice of a bestseller to review, '[*The Vanishing Half by* Brit Bennett] was plastered all over my instagram last year (at least for my algorithm). It was inescapable ☺ so I was aware that it was a bestseller but I did check the NY Times bestseller list to make sure and as expected it was there.'

For those who use social media to inform their book selections (all but one reader), certain titles become inescapable for the reasons that @chooks identifies. Indeed, in terms of preferred social media sources for book ideas, Instagram and YouTube, both with well-established reading recommendation cultures, were runaway favourites with our group. Their most-used platforms and apps were a mixture of sites where readers can post their own reviews (Goodreads, Amazon); apps that allow the formation of private chat groups or public groups (WhatsApp and WeChat; Facebook), and other social media platforms that offer forms of threaded discussion (Reddit). Their most-used sources were: Instagram (eleven; 68.8 per cent), YouTube (ten; 62.5 per cent), and Facebook (four; 25.0 per cent). For nine of the readers in the group, it is not uncommon for them to check their favourite reading-related platform once or twice a day; two readers check every couple of hours, and one reader consults it three or four times a day. Similar to the findings of Paramboukis, Skues, and Wise, whose study showed that 'the majority of Instagram users are consumers rather than creators of content' (2016, 86), the majority of the Gen Z readers (twelve; 75 per cent) are more likely to read posts than to make them. While checking and skim-reading posts on social media might at first appear passive, the readers in this group use their online reading recommendation sources in ways that can be understood as a form of 'public cultural engagement instead of participation because the former more appropriately captures the individual's prosumption agency as an initiator of cultural and communicative processes, not just placing him or her to a role of a participant of a pre-initiated process' (Jaakkola 2019, 93). For example, two readers cited different ways they used Instagram to find ideas for books to read, namely viewing 'recommendation lists curated by bookstagrammers to learn more about a topic' and 'secondhand book sellers on Instagram (ex: @literatereaders)'. One reader frequently uses StoryGraph, while another wrote, 'I have, in fact, deliberately tried to steer away from allowing social media to influence my reading.' This latter comment is a potent reminder that not all Gen Z readers who have ready access to networked social media choose to use it. Responding to reading recommendation culture may also, therefore, involve a deliberate refusal to engage with or employ certain aspects of it.

Responding to Bestsellers

I'm torn between two initial ideas that come to my mind when I read 'bestseller'. It's either 'NY Times bestseller' category (which I've ticked above) or it falls under the 'translated in different languages' and 'won many prizes' categor[ies]. I didn't want to tick both to avoid confusion. But I think the 'bestseller' recommendations I see on Instagram belong to the latter category. I've very rarely seen someone recommend a NY times kind of book. I see and read a lot of translated fiction that were bestselling in their countries. I think this is another benefit of Instagram, you see what you want to see. But I'll still stick to defining bestsellers as ticked above. (LPK, 25, Australia)

Nine members of the group indicated through the online questionnaire that they do read bestselling fiction, and seven readers reported that they did not usually do so. Among the bestsellers recently read by our readers were, in fact, a mixture of fiction and non-fiction genres. They identified books translated into English: Paulo Coelho's *The Alchemist*, which was mentioned by two readers; *Earthbound China*, which is a sociological study of the rural economy in Yunnan province; Memoirs (Michelle Obama's *Becoming*, Trevor Noah's *Born A Crime*); fiction that is part of a series (Lisa Maxwell's *The Last Magician*); a novel translated into more than forty languages (John Strelecky's *The Cafe on the Edge of the World*); and Celeste Ng's *Little Fires Everywhere*, winner of several prizes and the source for a television adaptation. Most of these bestsellers correspond with the various formal and popular definitions of 'bestseller' that we presented to readers in both of our online questionnaires. Determining what counts as a bestseller, however, was a more complicated process for the group, as the quotation suggests. For LPK, books that were successful in the author's home country, especially in terms of winning prizes, and which had then travelled internationally because they had been translated, were identifiably 'bestsellers'. Notably, this reader comments that Instagram's algorithm is potentially helpful in this regard because it delivers more of 'what you want to see'. For this reader, a bestseller appears to be a book that has accumulated some cultural legitimacy through various processes of consecration by traditional agents in the literary field, from prize jury members to publishers purchasing the translation rights. The visibility of some bestsellers recommended on Bookstagram – at least the ones that this reader is aware of – dovetails with these international, prize-winning profiles.

Contemplating what counts as a bestseller became an explicit part of the group conversation once we had asked readers to each select a work of bestselling fiction available in English published between 2019 and 2021 to read and review. We asked that the group share their process of selection in the group chat, and that, once they had read the book, they create a review of it on a social media platform of their choice. @bookswitadybug, an undergraduate student from Mauritius, turned to the group to help her assess whether sales volumes and rankings were an accurate means of identifying a bestseller. Her request and the subsequent conversation are in Figure 6.

In this part of the conversation, frau_lehrerin and @boingbellabooks combine their knowledge of how sales ranking systems can be manipulated by publishers with their research skills. Earlier in the exchange, frau_lehrerin shared links to two articles about how bestseller lists are compiled as part of her research for this task because she 'wanted to check [her] definition of bestselling books (= books with high sales figures)'. In exploring these issues about how various agents in the book industry can make a bestseller, and in their awareness of how algorithms can play a part in pushing sales of titles, these readers demonstrated both suspicion about the effects of marketing and about what counts as a bestseller, as well as

HavingFunWithReadingResearch
1 active today

Q Search Amazon

ISBN-13   Back to Top   1368

Item   7.5 ounces
Weight

Dimensions   5 x 0.7 x 8 inches

Best Sellers   #5,515,010 in Books (See
Rank   Top 100 in Books)
                #6,005 in Sociology of
                Marriage & Family (Books)
                #16,137 in Ethnic
                Demographic Studies
                #46,671 in Women's
                Biographies

Customer   4.4 out of 5 stars 38
Reviews   Reviews

Videos

Bella

Yeah, I agree, I don't usually look at bestseller lists when selecting books so actively choosing one is already making me more conscious/making me do more research in selection

I've worked with Amazon metadata for books before and publishers always try to find the most niche "genre" of a book possible so it can be considered a bestseller in that category and thus be treated nicely by the algorithm

This book that I'm interested in for example ranks at 5,515,010 in the best selling rank according to Amazon - Does that work? ☺

At the moment I'm looking at the UK overall top 50 & top 20 original fiction charts on thebookseller.com

frau_lehrerin

That's a good question 🤔 the article of the la editors and writers group mentions that "Amazon.com's rankings are even more fluid. The system that never sleeps bestows "Amazon bestseller" status to any book that edges into the top 100, even if only for a day." Guess this doesn't really help to answer your question, but it made me question again whether the term "bestseller" says anything about the quality of a book. ☺

 @bookswitadybug

Figure 6 'What is a bestseller?'

HavingFunWithReadingResearch
1 active today

This activity was exhausting! I
generally pick up books at
random, whatever catches my
fancy at the moment, and the
only time I'm selective is when
I'm adding to my collection of
old tattered books.

This was the first time ever
where I was really specific
about what I read and my brain
can't handle it 😵 I've been
through 150+ titles and around
4 bestseller lists.
It was difficult to pick just one,
I want to read them all!
(I should do this more often)

Figure 7 'This activity was exhausting!'

concerns about quality that resonate with the responses of readers in our large survey (see Section 2).

What is also evident here is the investment in the process of research itself: in their efforts to select a work of bestselling fiction in English, they became co-producers in our research about bestsellers. Figure 7 partially illustrates what Momo wrote in the chat.

Nonetheless, the results of their various investigations and their preferred online recommendation sources were not the only influences on their final choice. Energy levels, mood, the length of the book, and the amount of time available to them to read it, were some of the factors that informed the readers' decisions. Even if they had undertaken extra research to determine their choice, most readers combined the extra information they garnered with some of their usual selection practices. For LPK, who chose a Japanese bestseller translated into English, a category that she admits is her 'soft corner', indicated some initial hesitancy because 'it felt like a YA and had elements of fantasy, both [types of book that] I don't read much'. She decided after 'a bit more research from Good reads [*sic*] and also more bookstagrammers'. In this case, readers' reviews, trusted influencers, and an alignment with some aspects of her usual taste in fiction confirmed her decision. Mauritian reader @bookswitadybug used similar sources for her choice and explained how the book's paratexts – the cover, the summary, other readers' reviews – influenced her decision. She first saw *The Family Tree* by Sairish Hussain on Bookstagram, where 'it intrigued me because it spoke of family and relationships and life basically', so she 'checked the reviews on Goodreads (4.31/5) and decided that it was a good enough book for me to get into'. Like LPK, @bookswitaladybug trusts other readers' assessments as to whether this novel is worth her time. She is also critically self-aware that how a reader selects a book may indicate their readerly capital to others: 'the reason that pushed me to click on that particular book [on Bookstagram] was the book cover. They say not to judge a book by its cover, but sometimes we can't help getting attracted by what we first see [thinking emoji]'.

In South Africa, @essentialbird took a slightly different route by researching two authors he already admires, Chimamanda Ngozi Adichie and Jackie Phamotse. His initial hesitancy in picking Phamotse's book, *Bare: The Circle of the Hockey Club*, suggested the tension between feeling invested in an issue but also being aware that it might be emotionally difficult or even triggering to read a novel that examines it. @essentialbird wrote, 'my heart always wanted to read [Phamotse's] work, but her books covered topics that make me anxious and less excited, I guess, I wasn't ready to start an adventure that I knew it had so many emotions and hard things in it'. Similar concerns were shared within the group at several points over the eight weeks, with members alerting each other to content that might be potentially distressing because a book dealt with racism or homophobia and/or depicted some form of violence, for example. In doing so, the readers demonstrated a responsiveness and an ethics of care towards each other, as well as an awareness that their own lived experiences were differently informed by how they were racialized and gendered within their own societies.

The group's final choices ranged across subgenres of fiction; books written by writers from their own nation state and those that were not. Most of the selections were published by one of the big four publishers in English-language publishing and are owned by transnational media corporations, but several were not. Readers in Bangladesh (Ikra), Australia (LPK), and South Africa (@essentialbird), for example, all chose books published by companies outside of these media conglomerates. One reader borrowed their selection, while another used a pirated PDF: choices that were made although we had offered to pay for their book. In what they chose to read and in how they obtained their books the readers practiced some of the ethical, radical, and activist modes of 'careful consumption' outlined by Edmond (2022) as common among young adults.

Going against the Flow: Ethical Responsiveness

So here I am, using an American blog to look for South Asian Authors [shrugging emoji] and weirdly, it does a better job at representation than home-grown brands (Momo, 23, India).

Through their choosing practices, in-group book recommendations, and explanations about their selection of a bestselling work to review, our international group of Gen Z readers encountered and identified some of the barriers to and frictions within the transnational flow of goods, ideas and equitable representation within transnational bestsellers. Momo's declaration resulted from her extensive, yet fruitless search through '150+ titles and four bestseller lists' and her frustration with national news sources: 'I went through recommendations from Indian news houses too but the lists were *blah* (generic)', she commented. Her final choice, *Chats with the Dead* by Shehan Karunatilaka, a multiple award-winning Sri Lankan writer, was published by Penguin Random House India and later won the 2022 Booker Prize under its UK title, *The Seven Moons of Maali Almeida*. Momo uses the shrugging emoji to indicate the irony of using a blog (Huffpost) from the USA because it better represents South Asian authors than her local media sources. In fact, the irony extends further if we trace the political economy of her choice. The 'American blog' ultimately leads her to a novel published by the Indian subsidiary company of a US publishing house that is part of a German-owned media conglomerate, Bertelsmann.

What are the conditions under which a reader from the Global South goes on this type of recommendation journey? On the one hand, Momo, in common with other members of the group, was participating in reading recommendation cultures from Bookstagram to Goodreads reviews that are ostensibly international and transnational in terms of their circulation through networked reading cultures. English-language content, however, inevitably dominates within our group in terms of the online sources they use, because being able to read in English was a requirement set by our research parameters and by the original commission for this Element. Moreover, the dominance of the English language across regions of the world the British once colonized was made evident within a group of Gen Z readers that included an Indian, a Jamaican, two South Africans, a Mauritian, two Australians, and a Bangladeshi reader. Some of the group members located in the Global South also encountered the material effects of the imbalance of wealth between industrialized nation states in the Global North and their own nation states, when we sought to compensate them for their time through a thank-you gift of a book voucher. @chooks in Jamaica, for example, felt that she had no choice but to ask for an Amazon voucher, even though she prefers to buy from local bookstores. The constraints on her choice included the vast quantity of books that are shipped to the Caribbean from overseas versus locally published books, and the dominance of Amazon in that region. National banking regulations that prevented book voucher purchases on a Canadian credit card for readers located in Bangladesh and India also foregrounded how capital flows and money moves or, rather, are blocked from flowing and moving, around the world at the person-to-person level.

In contrast to these material constraints and structural inequalities, the readers demonstrated an ethics of responsiveness to each other and to how they understood themselves to be represented or under-represented in bestselling fiction in English. Their critical commentaries, when set alongside the economic conditions noted earlier, and copyright legislation (Sundara Rajan 2019) demonstrate the complications bound up in the term 'transnational'. As Hill (2019) reminds us, 'the transnational is a messy overlay of local, national and global, or intra-regional flows' (34). Our readers identified some of these 'messy overlays' and their effects on representation.

Conclusions

Readers' pathways through reading recommendations cultures, especially their use of social media platforms, illustrated how the type of under-representation they identify in terms of books that become bestsellers in English is often reproduced and recirculated through networked cultures of reading. The dominance of particular media outlets – especially Netflix and the *New York Times* – as vehicles not only for recommendations, but also as short-hands for quality media, is queried by this international group of readers, many of whom do not see their communities represented accurately in media products and on platforms owned and/or financed by companies in the Global North. The transnational networks of media subsidiary companies and, in particular, the 'branch plant' economies of the book industry, also shape what they see on their social media feeds and in their local bookstores. They continue to use these media, but they are critical of their power and conscious that algorithms play a role in the enactment of that power. While the local and national media that most of them also use in their daily lives offer news, fiction, and non-fiction that better represents their geopolitical situations and is produced in their first languages, this group of multilingual MMR[3]s participate in online reading communities both for pleasure *and* because of their ethical orientation towards the wider world. They have all found trusted others on Bookstagram or BookTube as well as among their friends, but these internationally dispersed readers are *also* aware of the failures of the publishing industry and media companies to address realities outside of northern Euro-American experiences. Their ethical responsiveness to the media ecologies and mediascapes they navigate presents a challenge, not only to English-language publishers and journalists, but also to the practices of book influencers, and, by extension, to the owners, managers, and coders of social media platforms. Most of our Instagram group members would probably join Jana at the event about inclusivity in publishing – and they would definitely have questions for the speakers.

5 Conclusion

For contemporary readers, bestsellers are just one type of book among many. If a particular bestseller coincides with their favourite author or genre, they are more likely to investigate the title. If a trusted friend or social media influencer recommends a bestseller, a reader is more likely to buy or borrow it. The simple result of our research is that the label of 'bestseller', whether it is symbolic or literal, is a navigational aid for many readers, one route to pursue – or to ignore – in figuring out their next book to read. As we have demonstrated in Sections 2 and 4, some readers will turn away from books that are explicitly promoted as 'bestsellers' because they want to resist the commercial 'hype' of marketing, whether it is made explicit in advertising copy or is more implicit in the algorithms shaping their social media feeds. Although bestselling fiction in English is often marketed as an 'international' commodity, these books sometimes fail to represent the communities and lived realities of large swathes of their supposedly 'global' audience. The dominance of US American agents of cultural production in terms of the books that become 'bestselling fiction' in English is apparent in the ownership of publishing houses, the largest of which have the capacity to harvest reader data, sponsor influential Bookstagrammers and BookTubers, and calibrate algorithms. The pervasiveness of US culture within anglophone book cultures is also signalled through the way that differently located readers in our study use the *New York Times* bestseller list as a lodestone. We also saw readers encountering this US cultural dominance within their wider twenty-first-century mediascapes where companies like Netflix and Amazon Prime remediate, recirculate, and (often but not always) reinforce the sales success of bestselling fiction titles.

Readers, however, are not merely passive agents of the anglophone book industry or of networked reading cultures. Both in our survey and again in our Instagram group, readers explicitly resisted US American books and sources of information about them. Some readers turned to influencers from their own nation state or region of the world, for example, or combined and compared reader reviews from Goodreads with the opinions of friends and family in their immediate social circles.

Respondents to our survey emphasized that in Sweden, Canada, and South Africa, to take just three examples, a 'bestseller' may not connote a particularly large volume of sales, and this knowledge disrupts the category of 'bestseller' for them, underscoring its unreliability as a measure not only of quality, but also of popularity in terms of audience and reach. These readers also offer a helpful reminder that the term 'bestselling fiction' can be conceptualized as situated and context-specific. Further, 'bestseller' signifies to some readers whose first language is not English as an 'anglo-centric' term. Some survey respondents reported the word or phrase used in their first language in resistance to the imperializing effects of English. Meanwhile, one effect of online recommendation culture is that readers understand more about how the publishing industry works than they did in the early 2000s. Most influencers working in the book-reading niches on social media platforms are clear about their connections to the industry, and readers can thus often identify when they are being presented with a paratext designed to prime them for engagement (Reinhard 2021, 280). Readers' accumulated knowledge of their own tastes and genre preferences, as well as those of trusted influencers, further assist decisions about choosing, connecting, and responding to prompts about bestsellers. Moreover, as Ariel comments, it is easier than ever for an avid reader to become more intensively involved in online reading recommendation culture, should they wish to do so:

> The low barrier to entry is one of the factors that has helped make YouTube so popular. The percentage of people who have access to a smartphone with a camera, or a laptop with a webcam, is already astonishingly high and is growing every day. Anyone over the age of 13 can have a YouTube account. And while the sky is the limit when it comes to how you edit your videos, in truth, none of it is necessary. There are many successful book channels that are filmed, edited, and maintained fully on a smartphone.

Even so, as researchers of contemporary cultures of reading who specialize in investigating reading as a social practice, we want to recognize rather than dismiss the tension between the power of media companies to harness aspects of networked reading cultures to make profit, and the agency of readers who are using or refusing online recommendation culture in a range of ways. We need to know more about how algorithms, data mining, and data surveillance operate and how managers at book publishing and media corporations use this data in their decision-making about which books to publish and which to market in and across different territories. Scholarship on patents and analyses of grey literature about platform technologies have begun that very necessary examination (Parnell 2022; Pianzola 2021; Rowberry 2022). But we also need studies that employ digital tools that can track at scale how a specific work of bestselling fiction moves across social media platforms, political economies of specific platforms regarding reading and book culture practices, and more critical scrutiny about modes of international distribution, including piracy.

Our starting point for *Reading Bestsellers* involved investigating readers' opinions about and relationships with bestselling fiction in English through three phases of mixed-methods research. However, even as we designed our quantitative survey, our enquiry became focussed on readers' engagement with recommendation culture. We wanted to elaborate some of the qualities of being a reader not just in a transmedia age, but in an era when old and new media, on- and offline practices, coexist. As we have demonstrated, especially in Sections 2 and 4, there is some continuity of practice with long-standing book recommendation and f2f book group habits: the differences, at the beginning of the third decade of the twenty-first century, are in scale, media, and sociality. The readers featured in all three sections of this Element demonstrate that reading sociality persists as a pleasurable aspect of the reading experience for many keen readers. For those who use the Internet to find information about books, to consult reader-to-reader reviews, and to respond through likes and emojis to others rather than creating their own posts or videos, their practices of sociality can be characterized as a form of light participation. Sociality in this mode is not interpersonal nor private, but rather a 'mass personal' means of communication (O'Sullivan & Carr 2018), a loose form of 'digital sociality' that is relatively undemanding in terms of a reader's time and energy but which nevertheless produces a sensation of connection. Certainly, some readers in our study, especially the influencers featured in Section 2 and some of the young adult readers in Section 4, also use online recommendation culture with more intent and variation: to quantify their reading, to display it, curate it, to demonstrate taste, and to engage in rivalry and play with other readers (Thomas 2020, 77).

Moreover, deeper, more bonded forms of relationship and community are possible within the online/offline spaces that recommendation culture on platforms make possible. Social media scholars have commented that Instagram, for instance, 'increasingly functions as a communication and commerce network, where sociality is template-based and communication rarely leads to collective experiences' (Tiidenberg, Hendry & Abidin 2021, 13). The influencers we interviewed for Section 2, however, articulated their affective attachment to groups of fellow influencer-readers, relationships they understood both as collegial and as friendships. Notably, those relationships sometimes become public online when influencers collaborate to produce content. These instances can be subject to co-option for profit and social capital: certainly, media companies benefit from their combined audience reach. But we can also see the influencers as avatars for other readers, offering a model not only for loving a book in public, but also for connecting as friends through that social practice. As such, the motivations and practices of influencers discussed in Section 2 do not always coincide with the features and affordances of the platforms that they use, nor with the demands of professionals in the book industries.

We encourage more research by reading studies scholars and contemporary book culture researchers into reader networks. In particular, how might we theorize the types of community that are explicit online and also those that are not? For example, what factors inform the formation, regulation, and practices of influencer-formed communities? What are the commonalities and differences across languages and regions, for example, between Bookstagrammers (Tselenti 2020)? Social media studies scholars have done some of this work for influencers working in areas like fashion, but there is little scholarship that takes up these issues in relation to book reading (see Martens et al. 2022). Rhodes (2022), for example, writes about Gen Z's fascination with and utilization of short-form media and Boffone and Herrera (2021) explain that social media platforms like Tiktok allow teens 'to feel a sense of belonging' (124). How does this operate for teenagers in relation to books and reading? Here, a turn to fan studies is helpful to analyze and conceptualize community formation. Moreover, as scholars of contemporary book culture, we must recognize that scenes of reading occur in various online spaces not only on BookTok, Bookstagram, and BookTube but also on reading/writing platforms like Wattpad and Archive of Our Own. Further, we noted in Section 2 that there is a recursive aspect of reading recommendation culture that occurs when an author indicates their approval and appreciation of an influencer's post about their book. That, combined with how successful BookTubers and Bookinstagrammers have published their own fiction books or aspire to do so, is an aspect of networked reading of interest to colleagues who research publishing and authorship.

One effect of networked reading communities that we have observed during this project is that being a keen reader, especially a fan of a specific genre, has become more visible as part of popular culture, and especially as an expression of 'geek culture'. The affective vocabulary used by readers on BookTok where 'crying', 'dying', and 'being shook' because of a specific book are deliberately dramatic expressions of reader response, is one example of this visibility and of the influence of other popular media on the language used within book recommendation culture (Ormonde 2022). Another significant element of being a reader in a transmedia era is the existence of bestselling fiction, especially YA and fantasy series, as 'transmedia property' (Martens 2019, 3). The creation and extension of storyworlds that are 'vast in their scope and minute in their detail' (Burek Pierce 2020, 214), offer opportunities for an extended immersive reading experience. While media companies aim to make megasellers out of specific properties, readers can prolong their enjoyment, not only by rereading but also by rewatching, and recirculating responses, whether through original content creation or via reblogging and reposting. These are all practices that we have identified as part of the repertoire of the multimodal reader cubed (MMR^3). Across the three sections of this minigraph we have attempted a nuanced examination of the MMR^3. We have made a distinction between influencers as MMR^3s *par excellence* and readers who read across formats, media, and devices but whose participation in terms of content creation online is minimal. Nevertheless, we also conceptualized such readers as MMR^{3}s. So, how generative a concept is this for reading studies? Very. We put readers and bestsellers at the centre of our investigation, but we did not differentiate between platforms or pay much attention to their specific features, functions, and affordances. What happens if we look more closely at reader practices on specific platforms not only via the published posts and rhetorical practices, but also through how platforms are linked via reader actions and cross-platform ownership? What about the Fediverse and semi-private reading groups on platforms like Discord? How do reader practices and communities in those spaces complicate or reconfigure the concept of the MMR^3?

Access to media and media technologies inform how the MMR^3 moves or does not move among on- and offline spaces, across their mediascape, and how or if they participate within communities of readers. Importantly, readers reminded us via their survey responses and in other phases of our research of not only their own preferences and practices, but also about social inequalities that they recognize and experience within reading recommendation cultures. Our multimodal, multilingual readers pushed back against the very categories of our research commission into reading bestselling fiction in anglophone markets. Some inequalities may be less visible to privileged readers, for example, a white cisgendered woman like our imagined character Sara. The ways that 'whiteness' shapes and dominates many reading communities and spaces online especially regarding taste formation (Dane 2023), and the toxicity of online spaces for racialized readers who encounter microaggressions are significant (Flanagan 2022). Further factors have come under critical scrutiny by scholars of digital media, such as the way white supremacy is upheld through the practices of coding (Benjamin 2019; Noble 2018; O'Neil 2016): the racialized skews in categorisation systems for books that make work by BIPOC writers more difficult to find when a reader searches online (Parnell 2022), and the failure of platform company managers to investigate complaints when the explicitly 'inclusive' ethics in their terms and conditions are transgressed (Parnell 2022). These are aspects of online reading cultures that readers who are privileged in terms of whiteness, class, location, and education do not have to think about very much, although if you asked them, they might well be supportive of social justice issues, have bookmarked anti-racist reading lists that appeared on their Instagram feed, and have a TBR pile that includes some of those titles. While ads on their social media feeds and suggestions of new readers to follow may make a privileged white reader wonder how algorithms are shaping what and who they encounter online, this does not guarantee any awareness of the ways that algorithmic culture reproduces the systemic inequalities of power from the offline world. The technological infrastructure of platforms, the capture of data about readers, and the ethics of for-profit organizations who own the platforms and use the data are among the less visible constraints inflecting readers' agency when they consult with aspects of online reading recommendation culture to choose their next book. These structuring/structural elements also require further examination if we are to thoroughly understand how readers encounter networked reading cultures online and offline. Finally, as readers in our survey and again in the Gen Z group reminded us, bestselling fiction in English should not consist primarily of books about 'boring, straight white people who create their own problems', or 'books that make white people feel good about themselves'. As readers have become more influential agents in the reading industry across the first decades of this century, book publishers particularly need to heed these demands.

As we imagine Sara, Priya, and Jana going about their everyday lives, snatching moments to read a book, create a Bookstagram post or podcast, or attend an event about publishing or an in-person author reading, recall the last bestseller that you read. How did you find out about it? What did you think? We guarantee that you can answer these questions because, even though no reader identifies bestsellers as their favourite type of book, most readers have an opinion about them.

References

Abidin, Crystal. 2015. 'Communicative ❤ Intimacies: Influencers and Perceived Interconnectedness'. *Ada New Media* (blog). 1 November. https://adanewmedia.org/2015/11/issue8-abidin.

Allington, Daniel, and Bethan Benwell. 2012. 'Reading the Reading Experience'. In *From Codex to Hypertext: Reading at the Turn of the Twenty-First Century*, edited by Anouk Lang, 217–33. Boston: University of Massachusetts Press.

Andersen, Christian Ulrik, Geoff Cox, and Georgios Papadopoulos. 2014. 'Postdigital Research'. *A Peer-Reviewed Journal about Rendering Research* 3 (1): 4–7. https://doi.org/10.7146/aprja.v3i1.116067.

Anderson, Porter. 2020. 'Coronavirus Impact: A New Survey by Italian Publishers Sees "Abandonment of Reading."' *Publishing Perspectives.* 16 July. https://bit.ly/3ZKH4Yl.

Archer, Jodie, and Matthew Lee Jockers. 2016. *The Bestseller Code: Anatomy of the Blockbuster Novel.* New York: St Martin's Press.

Armitstead, Claire. 2022. '"After Lockdown, Things Exploded": How TikTok Triggered a Books Revolution'. *The Guardian*, 8 June, sec. Books. http://bit.ly/3F2fDkW.

Auxier, Brooke, and Monica Anderson. 2021. 'Social Media Use in 2021'. *Pew Research Center: Internet, Science & Tech* (blog). 7 April. http://bit.ly/3kR2YdH.

Beale, Nigel. 2022. 'Kat McKenna on How Tiktok's BookTok Sells Books'. http://bit.ly/3F1ypZx.

Benjamin, Ruha. 2019. *Race after Technology: Abolitionist Tools for the New Jim Code.* Cambridge: Polity Press.

'Best Sellers – Books – The New York Times'. n.d. *New York Times.* www.nytimes.com/books/best-sellers.

Birke, Dorothee. 2021. 'Social Reading? On the Rise of a "Bookish" Reading Culture Online'. *Poetics Today* 42 (2): 149–72. https://doi.org/10.1215/03335372-8883178.

Boffone, Trevor, and Sarah Jerasa. 2021. 'Toward a (Queer) Reading Community: BookTok, Teen Readers, and the Rise of TikTok Literacies'. *Talking Points* 33 (1): 10–16.

BookNet Canada. 2020. 'Canadian Leisure and Reading Study 2020'. *BookNet Canada*. https://bit.ly/3IMRvUg.

    2022. 'The Real Impact of #BookTok on Book Sales'. *BookNet Canada*. http://bit.ly/3kSMrpu.

Boucher, Abigail, Chloe Harrison, and Marcello Giovanelli. 2020. 'How Reading Habits Have Changed during the Covid-19 Lockdown'. *The Conversation*. 5 October. http://bit.ly/3SR2HnA.

Bruns, Axel. 2008. *Blogs, Wikipedia, Second Life, and Beyond: From Production to Produsage*. New York: Peter Lang.

Burek Pierce, Jennifer. 2020. *Narratives, Nerdfighters, and New Media*. Iowa City: University of Iowa Press.

Burgess, Jean, and Joshua Green. 2018. *YouTube: Online Video and Participatory Culture*. Second edition. Cambridge: Polity.

Busse, Kristina. 2017. *Framing Fan Fiction: Literary and Social Practices in Fan Fiction Communities*. Iowa City: University of Iowa Press.

Butler, Richard J., Benjamin W. Cowan, and Sebastian Nilsson. 2005. 'From Obscurity to Bestseller: Examining the Impact of Oprah's Book Club Selections'. *Publishing Research Quarterly* 20 (4): 23–34. https://doi.org/10.1007/s12109-005-0045-2.

Chartier, Roger. 1992. 'Laborers and Voyagers: From the Text to the Reader'. *Diacritics* 22 (2): 49–61.

Chatelain, Marcia. 2019. 'Is Twitter Any Place for a [Black Academic] Lady?' In *Bodies of Information: Intersectional Feminism and the Digital*

Humanities, edited by Elizabeth Losh and Jacqueline Wernimont, 173–84. Minneapolis: University of Minnesota Press.

Childress, C. Clayton. 2011. 'Evolutions in the Literary Field: The Co-constitutive Forces of Institutions, Cognitions, and Networks'. *Historical Social Research / Historische Sozialforschung* 36 (3) (137): 115–35.

Collins, Jim. 2010. *Bring on the Books for Everybody: How Literary Culture Became Popular Culture*. Durham, NC: Duke University Press.

Cramer, Florien. 2014 'What Is "Post-Digital"?' *APRJA* 3 (1): 11–24. https://doi.org/10.7146/aprja.v3i1.116068.

Dane, Alexandra. 2023. *White Literary Taste Production in Contemporary Book Culture*. Elements in Publishing and Book Culture. Cambridge: Cambridge University Press. https://doi.org/10.1017/9781009234276.

Dane, Alexandra, and Millicent Weber, eds. 2021. *Post-digital Book Cultures: Australian Perspectives*. Clayton, VIC: Monash University Publishing.

Dietz, Laura. 2022. 'Projection or Reflection? The Pandemic Bookshelf As a Mirror for Self-Image and Personal Identity'. *English Studies* 103 (5): 675–89. https://doi.org/10.1080/0013838X.2022.2087034.

Driscoll, Beth. 2019. 'Book Blogs As Tastemakers'. *Participations* 16 (1): 280–305. www.participations.org/16-01-14-driscoll.pdf.

Driscoll, Beth, and DeNel Rehberg Sedo. 2018. 'Faraway, So Close: Seeing the Intimacy in Goodreads Reviews'. *Qualitative Inquiry* 25 (3): 248–59. https://doi.org/10.1177/1077800418801375.

Driscoll, Beth, and Claire Squires. 2020. *The Frankfurt Book Fair and Bestseller Business*. Elements in Publishing and Book Culture. Cambridge: Cambridge University Press. https://doi.org/10.10717/9781108933377.

Edmond, Maura. 2022. 'Careful Consumption and Aspirational Ethics in the Media and Cultural Industries: Cancelling, Quitting, Screening, Optimising'. *Media, Culture & Society* 45 (1): 92–107. https://doi.org/10.1177/01634437221099615.

English, James F. 2002. 'Winning the Culture Game: Prizes, Awards, and the Rules of Art'. *New Literary History* 33 (1): 109–35.

Fan, Alei, Han Shen, Laurie Wu, Anna S. Mattila, and Anil Bilgihan. 2018. 'Whom Do We Trust? Cultural Differences in Consumer Responses to Online Recommendations'. *International Journal of Contemporary Hospitality Management* 30 (3): 1508–25. https://doi.org/10.1108/IJCHM-01-2017-0050.

Faverio, Michelle, and Andrew Perrin. 2022. 'Three-in-Ten Americans Now Read E-books'. *Pew Research Center* (blog). 6 January. http://bit.ly/3YkPDrD.

Flanagan, Bronagh. 2022. *'To Me, Growing As a Person Is Really Important, and I Think Bookstagram Is Sort of Giving Me That Opportunity': A Qualitative Study of #bookstagram and Community-Building.* http://urn.kb.se/resolve?urn=urn:nbn:se:liu:diva-186437.

Flood, Alison. 2022. '"More Zeros Than I've Seen in My Life": The Author Who Got a Six-Figure Deal via "BookTok."' *The Guardian*. August 16, sec. Books. http://bit.ly/3IMpxYM.

Fuller, Danielle. 2019. 'Coda: The Multimodal Reader: Or, How My Obsession with NRK's *Skam* Made Me Think Again about Readers, Reading and Digital Media'. *Participations* 16 (1): 496–502. www.participations.org/16-01-23-fuller.pdf.

Fuller, Danielle, and DeNel Rehberg Sedo. 2023. '"It Was Plastered All Over My Instagram Last Year (At Least for My Algorithm)": Young Adult Readers and the Genres of Online Book Reviewing'. *Post45*. (forthcoming).

2013. *Reading beyond the Book: The Social Practices of Contemporary Literary Culture*. New York: Routledge.

Fuller, Danielle, DeNel Rehberg Sedo, and Claire Squires. 2011. 'Marionettes and Puppeteers? The Relationship between Book Club Readers and Publishers'. In *Reading Communities from Salons to*

Cyberspace, edited by DeNel Rehberg Sedo, 181–99. London: Palgrave Macmillan.

Gee, James Paul. 2004. *Situated Language and Learning: A Critique of Traditional Schooling*. First edition. Literacies. London: Routledge.

Gelder, Ken. 2019. *Adapting Bestsellers: Fantasy, Franchise and the Afterlife of Storyworlds*. Elements in Publishing and Book Culture. Cambridge: Cambridge University Press. https://10.1017/9781108 589604.

Ghosh, Anindita. 2003. *Power in Print: Popular Publishing and the Politics of Language and Culture in a Colonial Society, 1778–1905*. Vol. 6. New Delhi: Oxford University Press.

Gilbert, Julie, and Barbara Fister. 2011. 'Reading, Risk, and Reality: College Students and Reading for Pleasure'. *College & Research Libraries* 75 (5): 474–95. https://doi.org/10.5860/crl-148.

Goodrich, Kendall, and Marieke de Mooij. 2014. 'How "Social" Are Social Media? A Cross-Cultural Comparison of Online and Offline Purchase Decision Influences'. *Journal of Marketing Communications* 20 (1–2): 103–16. https://doi.org/10.1080/13527266.2013.797773.

The Handmaid's Tale. 2017. Daniel Wilson Productions, Littlefield Company, White Oak Pictures.

Harris, Elizabeth A. 2021. 'How Crying on TikTok Sells Books'. *New York Times*. 20 March, sec. Books. http://bit.ly/3ZLpmE0.

——— 2022. 'How TikTok Became a Best-Seller Machine', 1 July. http://bit.ly/41GY8jI.

Hill, Annette. 2019. *Media Experiences: Engaging with Drama and Reality Television*. London: Routledge.

Illouz, Eva. 2014. *Hard-Core Romance: 'Fifty Shades of Grey' Best-Sellers, and Society*. Chicago, IL: University of Chicago Press.

Jaakkola, Maarit. 2019. 'From Re-viewers to Me-viewers: The #bookstagram Review Sphere on Instagram and the Uses of the Perceived

Platform and Genre Affordances'. *Interactions: Studies in Communication & Culture* 10 (1/2): 91–110. https://doi.org/10.1386/iscc.10.1-2.91_1.

2022. 'Reviewing As Post-Institutional Cultural Production'. In *Reviewing Culture Online: Post-Institutional Cultural Critique across Platforms*, edited by Maarit Jaakkola, 61–81. Cham: Springer International.

Jenkins, Henry. 1992. *Textual Poachers Television Fans & Participatory Culture*. New York: Routledge.

Kim, Dorothy, TreaAndrea M. Russworm, Corrigan Vaughan, et al. 2018. 'Race, Gender, and the Technological Turn: A Roundtable on Digitizing Revolution'. *Frontiers: A Journal of Women Studies* 39 (1): 149–77.

Kirschenbaum, Matthew, and Sarah Werner. 2014. 'Digital Scholarship and Digital Studies: The State of the Discipline'. *Book History* 17 (1): 406–58. https://doi.org/10.1353/bh.2014.0005

Knibbs, Kate. 2020. 'The Coronavirus Pandemic Is Changing How People Buy Books'. *Wired*, 27 April. www.wired.com/story/coronavirus-book-sales-indie.

Konchar Farr, Cecilia. 2005. *Reading Oprah: How Oprah's Book Club Changed the Way America Reads*. Albany: State University of New York Press.

Krueger, Richard A., and Mary Anne Casey. 2009. *Focus Groups: A Practical Guide for Applied Research*. Los Angeles: Sage.

Leaver, Tama, Tim Highfield, and Crystal Abidin. 2020. *Instagram: Visual Social Media Cultures*. Cambridge: Polity Press.

Leavis, Q. D. 1977 (1932). *Fiction and the Reading Public*. Norwood, PA: Norwood Editions.

Long, Elizabeth. 2003. *Book Clubs: Women and the Uses of Reading in Everyday Life*. Chicago, IL: University of Chicago Press.

MacTavish, Kenna. 2021. 'The Emerging Power of the Bookstagrammer: Reading #bookstagram As a Post-digital Site of Book Culture'. In *Post-digital Book Cultures: Australian Perspectives*, edited by Alexandra Dane and Millicent Weber, 80–112. Melbourne: Monash University Publishing.

Marsden, Stevie. 2020. 'Literary Prize Culture'. *Oxford Research Encyclopedia of Literature*. https://doi.org/10.1093/acrefore/9780190201098.013.1030.

Martens, Marianne. 2019. *The Forever Fandom of Harry Potter: Balancing Fan Agency and Corporate Control*. Elements in Publishing and Book Culture. Cambridge: Cambridge University Press. https://doi.org/10.1017/9781108599092.

Martens, Marianne, Gitte Balling, and Kristen Higgason. 2022. '#BookTokMadeMeReadIt: Young Adult Reading Communities across an International, Sociotechnical Landscape'. *Information and Learning Sciences* 123 (11/12): 705–22. https://doi.org/10.1108/ILS-07-2022-0086.

McHenry, Elizabeth. 2002. *Forgotten Readers: Recovering the Lost History of African-American Literary Societies*. Durham, NC: Duke University Press.

McKinnon, J. Garrett. 2015. 'Adoption of E-Book Platform by Historical New York Times Best-Sellers: An Examination of the "Long Tail" Theory in Action'. *Publishing Research Quarterly* 31 (3): 201–14. https://doi.org/10.1007/s12109-015-9411-x.

Miller, Laura J. 2000. 'The Best-Seller List As Marketing Tool and Historical Fiction'. *Book History* 3 (1): 286–304.

Moorhead, John. 2010. 'Reading in Late Antiquity'. In *The History of Reading: A Reader*, edited by Shafquat Towheed, Rosalind Crone, and Katie Halsey, 52–65. London: Routledge.

Morley, David. 2021. 'Mobile Socialities: Communities, Mobilities and Boundaries'. In *The Routledge Handbook of Mobile Socialities*, edited by Annette Hill, Maren Hartmann, and Magnus Andersson, 22–37. New York: Routledge.

Murray, Conor. 2021. 'Tiktok Is Taking the Book Industry by Storm, and Retailers Are Taking Notice'. *NBC News*, 5 July, sec. Culture Matters. http://bit.ly/3L9qa1k.

Murray, Simone. 2011. *The Adaptation Industry: The Cultural Economy of Contemporary Literary Adaptation*. New York: Routledge.

⸻ 2018. *The Digital Literary Sphere: Reading, Writing, and Selling Books in the Internet Era*. Baltimore, MD: Johns Hopkins University Press.

⸻ 2019. 'Secret Agents: Algorithmic Culture, Goodreads and Datafication of the Contemporary Book World'. *European Journal of Cultural Studies* (24) 4: 970–89. https://doi.org/10.1177/1367549419886026.

Noble, Safiya Umoja. 2018. *Algorithms of Oppression: How Search Engines Reinforce Racism*. New York: New York University Press.

Noorda, Rachel, and Kathi Inman Berens. 2021. 'Final Immersive Media Report'. Portland, OR. https://bit.ly/3YrZBaX.

'Nordic Embassy – International Business Development Consultancy'. n.d. Nordic Embassy – International Business Development Consultancy. https://nordic-embassy.com.

Norrick-Rühl, Corinna, and Shafquat Towheed, eds. 2022. *Bookshelves in the Age of the COVID-19 Pandemic*. London: Palgrave Macmillan.

O'Neil, Cathy. 2016. *Weapons of Math Destruction: How Big Data Increases Inequality and Threatens Democracy*. New York: Crown.

Ormonde, Ismene. 2022. 'Inspirational Passion or Paid-For Promotion: Can BookTok Be Taken on Face Value?' *The Guardian*, 15 November, sec. Books. http://bit.ly/3mtP8P1.

O'Sullivan, Patrick B., and Caleb T. Carr. 2018. 'Masspersonal Communication: A Model Bridging the Mass-Interpersonal Divide'. *New Media & Society* 20 (3): 1161–80. https://doi.org/10.1177/1461444816686104.

Ouvry-Vial, Brigitte. 2019. 'Reading Seen As a Commons'. *Participations* 16 (1): 141–73. www.participations.org/16-01-09-ouvry.pdf.

Paramboukis, Olga, Jason Skues, and Lisa Wise. 2016. 'An Exploratory Study of the Relationships between Narcissism, Self-Esteem and Instagram Use'. *Social Networking* 5 (2): 82–92. https://doi.org/10.4236/sn.2016.52009.

Parnell, Claire. 2022. Platform Publishing in the Entertainment Ecosystem: Experiences of Marginalised Authors on Amazon and Wattpad. PhD. Melbourne: University of Melbourne. https://trove.nla.gov.au/work/250480152.

Parnell Claire, and Beth Driscoll. 2021. 'Institutions, Platforms and the Production of Debut Success in Contemporary Book Culture'. *Media International Australia*, August. https://doi.org/10.1177/1329878X211036192.

Peplow, David, Joan Swann, Paola Trimarco, and Sara Whiteley. 2015. *The Discourse of Reading Groups: Integrating Cognitive and Sociocultural Perspectives*. London: Routledge.

Pianzola, Federico. 2021. *Digital Social Reading: Sharing Fiction in the 21st Century*. Cambridge, MA: MIT Press.

Pressman, Jessica. 2021. *Bookishness: Loving Books in a Digital Age*. New York: Columbia University Press.

2014. *Digital Modernism: Making It New in New Media, Modernist Literature & Culture*. New York: Oxford University Press.

Radway, Janice. 1991. *Reading the Romance: Women, Patriarchy, and Popular Literature*. Chapel Hill: University of North Carolina Press.

Ramdarshan Bold, Melanie. 2019. 'Is "Everyone Welcome"? Intersectionality, Inclusion, and the Extension of Cultural Hierarchies on Emma Watson's Feminist Book Club, Our Shared Shelf'. *Participations* 16 (1): 441–72. www.participations.org/16-01-21-ramdarshan.pdf.

Reddan, Bronwyn. 2022. 'Social Reading Cultures on BookTube, Bookstagram, and BookTok'. *Synergy* 20 (1). http://slav.vic.edu .au/index.php/Synergy/article/view/597.

Reichelt, Leisa. 2007. 'Ambient Intimacy'. *Disambiguity* (blog). 1 March. www.disambiguity.com/ambient-intimacy.

Reinhard, CarrieLynn. 2021. 'The Case for Media Engaging(s): Or, How I Learned to Be Both/and in an Either/or Discipline'. *Participations* 18 (1): 274–98. www.participations.org/18-01-16-reinhard.pdf.

Rhodes, Cris. 2022. 'Anthologizing Activism: Short Stories' Role in Fostering Reading and Inciting Revolution'. Paper presented at YA Studies Association Conference, Digital, October.

Rodger, Nicola. 2019. 'From Bookshelf Porn and Shelfies to #bookfacefriday: How Readers Use Pinterest to Promote Their Bookishness'. *Participations* 16 (1): 473–95. www.participations.org/16-01-22-rodger.pdf.

Rowberry, Simon. 2022. *Four Shades of Gray*. Cambridge, MA: MIT Press. https://doi.org/10.7551/mitpress/11985.001.0001.

  2019. 'The Limits of Big Data for Analyzing Reading'. *Participations* 16 (1): 237–57. www.participations.org/16-01-12-rowberry.pdf.

Scott, Suzanne. 2019. *Fake Geek Girls: Fandom, Gender, and the Convergence Culture Industry*. New York: New York University Press.

Serafini, Frank. 2012. 'Expanding the Four Resources Model: Reading Visual and Multi-modal Texts'. *Pedagogies: An International Journal* 7 (2): 150–64. https://doi.org/10.1080/1554480X.2012.656347.

Smith, Michael D., and Rahul Telang. 2016. *Streaming, Sharing, Stealing: Big Data and the Future of Entertainment*. Cambridge, MA: MIT Press.

So, Richard Jean. 2021. *Redlining Culture: A Data History of Racial Inequality and Postwar Fiction*. New York: Columbia University Press. https://doi.org/10.7312/so—19772.

Sorensen, Alan T. 2017. 'Bestseller Lists and the Economics of Product Discovery'. *Annual Review of Economics* 9: 87–101. https://doi.org/10.1146/annurev-economics-080614-115708.

Squires, Claire. 2004. 'A Common Ground? Book Prize Culture in Europe'. *Javnost: The Public* 11 (4): 37–47. https://doi.org/10.1080/13183222.2004.11008866.

2020. 'Essential? Different? Exceptional? The Book Trade and Covid-19. *C21: Journal of Twentieth-Century Writings*. 10 December. https://c21.openlibhums.org/news/403.

2021. 'Highland Flings and CAN CANs: Dances with Recommendation Culture'. *Scottish Literary Review* 13 (2): 91–115.

Steiner, Ann. 2014. 'Serendipity, Promotion, and Literature: The Contemporary Book Trade and International Megasellers'. In *Hype: Bestsellers and Literary Culture*, edited by Jon Helgason, Sara Kärrholm, and Ann Steiner, 55–90. Lund: Nordic Academic Press.

Still Watching Netflix, dir. 2021. *BookTubers React to Shadow and Bone | Don't Mess This Up | Netflix*. www.youtube.com/watch?v=CwmHxPedOPs.

Sundara Rajan, Mira T. 2019. 'Copyright and Publishing: Symbiosis in the Digital Environment'. In *The Oxford Handbook of Publishing*, edited by Angus Phillips and Michael Bhaskar, 71–83. Oxford: Oxford University Press.

Sutherland, John. 2007. *Bestsellers: A Very Short Introduction*. Oxford: Oxford University Press.

Thomas, Bronwen. 2021. 'The #bookstagram: Distributed Reading in the Social Media Age'. *Language Sciences* 84 (March). https://doi.org/10.1016/j.langsci.2021.101358.

2020. *Literature and Social Media*. London: Routledge. https://doi.org/10.4324/9781315207025.

Tiidenberg, Katrin, Natalie Ann Hendry, and Crystal Abidin, Crystal. 2021. *Tumblr*. Cambridge: Polity.

TikTok. 2022. 'It's Time to Join the TikTok Book Club! | TikTok Newsroom'. 18 July. https://newsroom.tiktok.com/en-gb/the-tik tok-bookclub.

Tselenti, Danai. 2020. '"What a Nice Picture!" Remediating Print-Based Reading Practices through Bookstagram.' Conference paper. Digital Practices: Reading, Writing and Evaluation on the Web. University of Basel, Switzerland, 23–25 November.

Van Dijck, Jose. 2013. *The Culture of Connectivity: A Critical History of Social Media*. Oxford: Oxford University Press.

Weber, Millicent. 2019. 'On Audiobooks and Literature in the Post-digital Age'. *Overland Literary Journal*, October. http://bit.ly/3kYOEQh.

Wiederhold, Brenda K. 2022. 'BookTok Made Me Do It: The Evolution of Reading'. *Cyberpsychology, Behavior, and Social Networking* 25 (3): 157–8. https://doi.org/10.1089/cyber.2022.29240.editorial.

Wilkins, Kim, Beth Driscoll, and Lisa Fletcher. 2022. *Genre Worlds: Popular Fiction and Twenty-First-Century Book Culture*. Boston: University of Massachusetts Press.

Wilkins, Kim, and Lisa Fletcher. 2021. *Writing Bestsellers: Love, Money, and Creative Practice*. Elements in Publishing and Book Culture. Cambridge: Cambridge University Press. https://doi.org/10.1017/9781108663724.

Yin, Robert K. 2017. *Case Study Research and Applications: Design and Methods*. New York: Sage.

Young, Liam. 2017. *List Cultures: Knowledge and Poetics from Mesopotamia to BuzzFeed*. Amsterdam: Amsterdam University Press.

Zappavigna, Michele. 2011. 'Ambient Affiliation: A Linguistic Perspective on Twitter'. *New Media & Society* 13 (5): 788–806. https://10.1177/1461444810385097.

Acknowledgements

We would like to thank R. Allana Bartlett, Emma MacMillan and Shivaughn King for their excellent work as research assistants, and the University of Alberta and Mount Saint Vincent University for funding this project.

Cambridge Elements ≡

Publishing and Book Culture

SERIES EDITOR

Samantha Rayner
University College London

Samantha Rayner is Professor of Publishing and Book Cultures at UCL. She is also Director of UCL's Centre for Publishing, co-Director of the Bloomsbury CHAPTER (Communication History, Authorship, Publishing, Textual Editing and Reading) and co-Chair of the Bookselling Research Network.

ASSOCIATE EDITOR

Leah Tether
University of Bristol

Leah Tether is Professor of Medieval Literature and Publishing at the University of Bristol. With an academic background in medieval French and English literature and a professional background in trade publishing, Leah has combined her expertise and developed an international research profile in book and publishing history from manuscript to digital.

ABOUT THE SERIES

This series aims to fill the demand for easily accessible, quality texts
available for teaching and research in the diverse and dynamic fields
of Publishing and Book Culture. Rigorously researched and
peer-reviewed Elements will be published under themes, or
'Gatherings'. These Elements should be the first check point for
researchers or students working on that area of publishing and book
trade history and practice: we hope that, situated so logically at
Cambridge University Press, where academic publishing in the UK
began, it will develop to create an unrivalled space where these
histories and practices can be investigated and preserved.

Cambridge Elements ≡

Publishing and Book Culture

Bestsellers

Gathering Editor: Beth Driscoll

Beth Driscoll is Associate Professor in Publishing and
Communications at the University of Melbourne. She is the
author of *The New Literary Middlebrow* (Palgrave Macmillan,
2014), and her research interests include contemporary reading
and publishing, genre fiction and post-digital literary culture.

Gathering Editor: Lisa Fletcher

Lisa Fletcher is Professor of English at the University of
Tasmania. Her books include *Historical Romance Fiction:
Heterosexuality and Performativity* (Ashgate, 2008) and *Popular
Fiction and Spatiality: Reading Genre Settings*
(Palgrave Macmillan, 2016).

Gathering Editor: Kim Wilkins

Kim Wilkins is Professor of Writing and Deputy Associate
Dean (Research) at the University of Queensland. She is also
the author of more than thirty popular fiction novels.

Printed in the United States
by Baker & Taylor Publisher Services